TABLE o

1

FOREWORD

In war everything has a bearing on the peace that must follow. This book is no exception. It presents many a phase of the past which may serve as a lesson for the future.

August 1942

When in 1922 the late Frank Andrew Munsey became my master by right of purchase of the *Herald* newspaper, and he asked with studied curtness: "What are you?" I replied almost as curtly: "French by birth, English by education, American by vocation." He said: "Ha!" And there ended our first conversation.

Were it possible again to enact the scene, I should be tempted to retort: "I am a product of what once were styled 'The Three Great Democracies'." Whereto he would probably say: "Ugh!" For, self-made man though he was, Munsey as I knew him was no democrat. Possibly that explains why he went to his grave unhonoured and unwept. In any case my hypothetical answer explains why this book was originally conceived. A war, an armistice and the rise of the United Nations brought many delays and compelled many modifications.

It shows in passing that there are men – women too, for that matter – who have become thoroughly American in speech, in manner and in outlook without losing their original nationality, indeed while remaining sensitively loyal to it. I am of the number; there are thousands of others. We form a 49th State, without the Union. And we imagine – fondly perhaps –

that we are not without influence on our fellows. In any case, so far as I am concerned, my life-story seems to prove that a Frenchman can be also an American newspaperman.

At the same time this book describes a long quest, triple in appearance yet single in purpose; an exploration in search of liberty, of democracy and of comprehension of America. Can the three be combined? Are liberty and democracy synonymous? Where did America stand? And what will be her part when Peace returns to the sorely tried world?

There is another aspect. My own life spans approximately that of the Third Republic in France, the regime which fell in June 1940. I saw its rise and I was present at its fall. The story should be a lesson for the future. For France Eternal will rise again.

I must confess at the outset that one part of my quest has been at long range. Circumstances have so ordered that despite wanderings on several continents I have yet to set foot on American soil. When opportunities did present themselves, various reasons intervened to keep me in Europe; one publisher at least feared that if I crossed the Atlantic I might never return. Probably he was right.

Therefore my knowledge of America is that of an armchair Columbus. Yet in the course of long service, both as editor and correspondent, I have helped to form scores of young American newspapermen and I have striven, not without success I believe, to interpret to America that Europe which has now disappeared.

Of necessity this book is autobiographical in major part, not because my own story has any interest, but because of the men I have known, the historic sights I have seen and the many things I have noted. Some chapters, for instance, were written in 1939 "on the Western Front" not far from the Maginot Line, when war, the very negation of liberty, shaped many a destiny, changed many an outlook. I shall endeavour nevertheless to remain in the background, leaving the footlights to others.

Also, I endeavour to be objective. Bias precludes comprehension. Especially in considering liberty and democracy, it is too easy to be swayed by sentiment, to assume that the label correctly describes the content. Furthermore, words cannot replace entities. Constitutions or fundamental laws may proclaim: "In this land men are free" or "Our form of government is democratic". Speakers from their rostrums may repeat this to satiety. It is not enough. There should be experimental proof. And experimental proof calls for inquiry, research and observation. That has ever been my main purpose. Not that in youth I began this quest deliberately. As with most human endeavours, this one took shape by degrees. For that reason the narrative follows no plan; above all, it cannot be tied to chronology. The reader will find it disconnected. May he be indulgent.

It may be well at the outset to define the political philosophy of the author. Memories of the Great Revolution overshadowed the destiny of every French lad of my generation. Already those memories were hazy. Yet they sufficed to instill a craving for liberty, above all liberty of thought. Random reading, Eugène Delacroix' painting in the Louvre of frock-coated bourgeois and blouse worker on a barricade by the side of a guttersnipe beating a drum while Liberty holds the Tricolour on high, Honoré Daumier's heartrending lithograph of political repression in the form of the dead in the Rue Transnonain, many another factors, all tended to the same end – to make each youth a revolutionary, a contemptor of orthodoxy. So did in my case acquaintance, on the British side, with John Hampden and the Chartists; on the American side, with the Boston tea party, Paul Revere and the Minutemen.

One hero of my youth, unavowed in middle-class surroundings, was Auguste Blanqui. Not that I knew much of this life-long conspirator who passed the greater part of his years in prison cells. He appealed because of his seeming disinterestedness and steadfastness, because of the devotion to a cause even if that cause remained obscure. In later years, it is true, study of his life and times cast doubt on his sincerity, but the impression remained vivid. It seemed a glorious thing to go into the street with a musket, there to oppose tyranny in its every form and, if need be, to die to make men free. Insurgency appealed as the only noble ideal, though what would come from insurrection remained murky.

The Commune of 1871, too, had left its impress on many young minds. As a child I had heard in the family circle endless tales of those weeks of civil war and street fighting under the very eyes of the victorious Prussian encircling Paris. The open-air dealers in second-hand books on the banks of the Seine still offered for sale volumes and pamphlets on the Commune. I had read many. I reproved at the same time the excesses of the Communards and the ruthless repression by the Government. I despised those leaders whose only concern was to strut in gaudy uniforms and, after defeat, to flee ignominiously. My admiration went to those who had died for their convictions, to old Charles Delescluze, for instance, who when all was lost climbed atop the barricade under a hail of lead. There was Jourde also, who administered the finances of the movement. Though a poor man, he accounted for every penny in the Bank of France and distrained only two dollars a day for his salary, while Madame Jourde continued to go down to the river to wash his clothes. Many Blanquists had fought for the Commune, humble men for the most part, earnest and honest – and brave when facing the firing squad. They, certainly, represented the People.

The Commune, incidentally, holds more than retrospective interest today. Communards must not be confused with Communists. They were Federalists. Their scheme of government, it must be confessed, was never very clear even to themselves, and their ranks were swollen by many adventurers and fishers in troubled waters, not to speak of jailbirds, none of whom cared a rap about political systems. With reminiscences of medieval guilds and free cities, the idea was to make the commune or community the basic unit in a federated state. Indeed it would not be too far-fetched, though disproportionate, to draw a parallel between this conception of communal rights and that of States Rights in America. In any case the fact is worth recalling at a time when some see the salvation of mankind in a federation of the world. Moreover, and paradoxically enough, there is in all this the germ of the authoritarian corporative idea evolved by Benito Mussolini, Adolf Hitler – and Philippe Pétain.

As years passed, however, more knowledge came from the frequentation of men, high and low. And things no longer seemed so simple. Youthful impulse attuned itself to surroundings. Experience has a sobering effect, even on Blanquism. Barricades appeared as a figure of speech instead of a reality when history showed that too often they were defended by the rank and file rather than by leaders. Yet the craving for liberty has never died, though doubts have entered the mind regarding a definition of democracy.

In these pages, Republican France will serve repeatedly as an example, with a moral to be drawn from her fall. The depth of that fall can be gauged only by those who, in June 1940, were caught in the Great Exodus. One needs to have lived through it to understand how humanity can become derelict, leaderless, hopeless, reason-less. That experience will ever haunt my memory. It so obviously marked the end of an epoch.

The Great Exodus left its mark on every man, woman and child caught in it, straws borne on a torrent.

It left its mark on France also, outranking both war and defeat. The apathy which it bred explains the Armistice of June 22, 1940, and much that followed. It explains the Pétain regime, with its policy of "wait and see"; it explains the abject rush for German gold under the guise of "collaboration" – gold which in reality was French; it explains Pierre Laval who, at the time of writing, is nearer each day to his inexorable end, when his white tie will serve as a noose and gadflies will swarm on his blackened tongue.

As the crossing of the Red Sea dominates the history of Israel, so the Great Exodus dominates that of contemporary France. It so exceeds all other incidents of my own life that it stands first in my recollections. I feared for a time that had ended my quest. But after many months of anguish hope rose again. Spontaneously and though leaderless France cast off apathy and found a new soul. For she knew that she must live – for Liberty, for Democracy!

CHAPTER 1

HITLER TAKES THE HINDMOST

Fifty years hence perhaps the story of the Great Exodus may be told, with continuity and perspective. For the moment it stands in most minds as a nightmare, blurred, chaotic, awful. Yet the definitive narrative of future historians will be but the sum of individual impressions. Here are mine:-

When in May 1940 the Germans entered Holland and Belgium, the most timorous fled South forthwith; others followed as fast as the enemy advanced. There was a lull while eyes were riveted on Dunkirk. In June it became panic. Millions upon millions were seized with the Great Fear.

With bedding lashed to the roofs to serve as protection against bullets, thousands of automobiles set out, filled with all that could be crammed into them – men, women and children, cats, dogs and canary birds, food, drink and clothing. Others rode away on bicycles, also in thousands. Still others went afoot. All carried what they possibly could. Railroad trains were packed; so long were the waiting lines that it took hours to buy a ticket. Every road was a compact mass of terrified humanity. In the majority of cases the fugitives had no set destination; they merely headed South, ever South.

Each day the exodus increased. When Paris joined the mad rush it seemed as if all France were on the move. To stem the tide the Government had ordained that from June 10 no one could travel without a safe-conduct. As with most of its enactments, the words had no weight. By the irony of fate, the Government itself left the capital that very day. Who cared about safe-conducts? Who cared about the Government? No force on earth could have stemmed the human torrent. Everyone for himself and the devil – or Hitler – takes the hindmost!

June 10 came exactly one month after the Germans had entered the Low Countries. The day before, Jean Prouvost, wool spinner and newspaper publisher, just pitchforked into the Ministry of Information, had sent for American correspondents. This was the news he gave: "Gentlemen, we shall defend Paris street by street, house by house. And when you want me you will find me here, right in this building." Bravo words! But everything gave Prouvost the lie. As the correspondents went downstairs they met scores of men loading typewriters and office furnishing into trucks for the flight next day.

The correspondents followed the Government in its peregrinations – to Tours, to Bordeaux, to Clermont-Ferrand, to Vichy. They too became refugees, joining millions of others of all nationalities. Among the first to flee were those who had fled before, even as far back as the other war – White Russians, anti-Fascist Italians, Czechs, Slovaks, Poles, Jews. Now it was the turn of Dutch, Belgians, French.

Never had there been such migration. Seldom fewer than three abreast, sometimes as many as five or six, cars and trucks moved along the roads with scarce an interval between. Whenever the file was halted for any reason – a sporadic attempt to regulate traffic, a collision or what not – the flow ceased for a minute or an hour. When it ran again, its volume had increased still more. Of necessity, the movement was irregular, for there were farm wagons also, drawn by plodding plough-horses and bearing strange loads – hay and oats for the teams, coops crammed with poultry and rabbits. Wizened gaffers and gammers in Sunday black and beaver hats or white

11

bonnets watched the throng overtake them; wide-eyed children sat on their laps. In and out of the vehicles cyclists weaved their way. For relative safety, those on foot walked by the roadside; among them were many mothers pushing baby carriages. The string of baby carriages rent one's heart.

The refugees afoot were most pathetic of all. Despite their anxiety and their cargoes of household chattels, those in automobiles still retained something of Sunday picnic parties. Those on bicycles, mostly young folk or man and wife on a tandem, recalled vacation days with their tents and frying pans. But the trudging mass! Men, women, children of all ages, footsore and dust-stained. Terror had urged them forth, and terror was written on every face. Very soon they wearied, but still they pushed on, with slow automatic gait, tragic parodies of children's mechanical toys.

Haggard women harnessed themselves to contraptions of rough boards and bicycle wheels, or simply slung babe in shawls. Men groaned under loads of bedding and loaves of bread and cans of food. At nightfall, utterly exhausted, with blistered feet and soles falling from worn shoes, they huddled on bare floors or on the roadside. Dawn saw some who could not rise. The line of flight became a long graveyard. But the law of Nature is inexorable; there were births as well as deaths.

All were bound for a haven of peace and quiet. Each morn was full of hope, each eve filled with anxiety, doomed to perpetual motion. The highway became the only home, with the ditch for bed or tomb. Each road had its endless funereal procession. Occasionally German airplanes droned overhead, even some Italian. Then the roads were stilled, with all seeking safety in the fields or woods. A village clock striking the hour sounded as a dirge. A child moaned "Mummy! I don't want to die!" Rain and lowering skies would have befitted the scene; to mark the irony, the sun had never been so bright.

12

There was not much dust on tarred roads, but the air seemed thick with the noise of grinding brakes and gripping tyres. And there was an all-pervading reek of gasoline, oil and perspiration. Whenever the column halted the silence was haunting. For in this flowing tide few words passed, apart from muttered oaths at the never-ceasing stop and go, stop and go, or shouts of anger when any left the line in a rash attempt to sneak ahead. Some faces were tense, even awed; others seemed horror-stricken. Yet the prevailing note was selfish apathy. The reporter thought not of taking notes, nor the photographer of snapping his camera. The only thought was to go faster, ever faster. For wild stories ran along the columns - of bombs and machine-guns and atrocious sights: bodies laid out in rows, with mothers still clasping babes.

There were other stories also, sprung from nowhere. "The radio gave it out ten minutes ago. Russia has declared war on Germany and Italy. All the Balkan countries are in the fight." None questioned the source – but next morning the newspapers were dumb on the matter. Then it was remembered that automobiles, remarkable because not travel-scarred, had darted out from side roads. Men standing in them raised placards: "Russia is in the war! Workers turn back at once! The shops are reopening!" Possibly the Fifth Column was busy. But none turned back. The tide flowed on, and on, and on.

Each noon there was a lull. One after another, cars halted by the wayside: time to eat. Cold ham, garlic sausages and red wine; then a litter of greasy paper, empty cans and bottles. Bakeries and wine shops were stormed. Soon signs appeared in the villages: "No more bread! No more gasoline!" Before taking the road again gaping groups stood to see the stream pass. France divided into two parts – those who rushed by and those who watched the rush. Towards sunset, another lull for another meal and preparations for slumber. In every town and village hotels and inns were packed; so the majority slept as best it could. Some had brought tents; others wrapped in blankets dozed restlessly in their cars or in the fields; yet others took advantage of clear roads to push on all night. At dawn the full stream flowed on again.

The most striking characteristic of that stream was that every man, woman and child had brought a gas mask. Not one had thought of leaving it behind. Indeed the mask had become the true symbol of a war which for eight months had remained "funny", to turn suddenly tragic. In the early days of September people had waited hours in line when masks were issued. Most air-raid shelters were illusory; many people did not even trouble to go there when sirens screeched. Not one inhabitant of Paris in a thousand but disregarded ordinances enjoining that sand should be ready to extinguish fires; no one bothered to remove inflammable material from attics. Most other regulations remained a dead letter. But all clung to the mask as a sort of fetish.

On the second day of my journey South the sky was darkened by what seemed at first an unseasonable mist. Men emerged from it with smudged faces. Greasy particles floated in the air – likely lamp-black. The sun was sinister in that fog. None could explain. Next day papers spoke of smoke-screens laid by the Germans while they bridged the Seine: later there was talk of flaming gasoline and petroleum tanks. We had driven about an hour when out of the smoky pall a man on a bicycle passed us. Hatless, he pedalled for very life. Sweat oozed through the film of black on his face; his eyes reflected absolute terror. Alone among the fleeing mob he had no baggage at all. But a gas mask, slung over his shoulder, swayed from side to side. Occasionally a hand would jerk it back from the knees in automatic gesture. I recognised the clerk from the grocery store who called at our house for the weekly order. He did no see me; obviously he saw nothing but the path of escape

14

he must follow. France was prepared against poison gas; poison gas was the sole mode of warfare not used!

The flight continued for days. More to the North, the stream of refugees had impeded the march of Army columns and convoys. South of Paris one saw no troops in any number, apart from Regional Regiments composed of elderly men whose mission was to guard communications rather than engage battle. We met isolated British Tommies living in tents, ready to pot at parachutists or to signal the appearance of enemy airplanes. They welcomed a tot of whisky, then with a grin resumed their vigil. Once we ran into a motorised brigade, or it might have been a division – brand new trucks filled with infantry, towing anti-tank and anti-aircraft guns, all spick and span, with motorcyclists dashing headlong in and out of the column. It looked very efficient. But it turned out to be a Polish unit and it, too, was heading south. The truth began to dawn upon one: the French had no more reserves. Faster still went the stream.

After most of the refugees had passed, the exodus became military. Hospital formations, artillery and other parks, stragglers from the firing line, men of all arms filled the roads in their turn. Behind them troops fought delaying actions, many heroic but all to no avail. Soon retreat was the only hope at every point.

Then the exodus came to its full horror. In hopeless medley soldier and refugee vied in speed. Fear grew hourly as bombs did their work, invisible but ever-present. Flight had turned into rout; rout turned into panic. The stream would engulf a village, only to turn back and confound confusion, because of houses aflame and dead horses already stinking to high heaven. And the roads were strewn with litter indescribable, arms and equipment mingling with birdcages, bedding and underwear. The rout was proved sufficiently by the

15

number of derelict trucks, cars, even cannon on the roadside when, after the Armistice, the stream turned about from South to North, each refugee this time seeking the haven of home. But there were many obstacles to surmount before crossing into the zone occupied by the Germans (by that time definitions had changed; it was no longer "the enemy" but "the adversary"). So that there were more breadlines, more meals by the roadside, more sleeping in fields. Gasoline had become priceless. Already on the way out it had become difficult to obtain. At each filling station people waited for hours, only too frequently to no purpose. Many encamped there for the night, still hoping for the coming of a tank-car. Few slept, for fear of thieves syphoning their remaining fuel. Soon the military authority took control of distribution – most sparingly. Yet cars with Army number-plates careered along all roads, often empty of passengers, or in the towns carried non-combatant officers and their ladies – to go shopping or merely to take the air. It was so scandalous that commanders strove to react. On main highways posts were instructed to halt all Army vehicles and ascertain the identity and business of the occupant.

So, for more than three months, France turned nomadic in dire circumstance. In great measure the flight could have been avoided, particularly south of the Loire. People who remained in their village homes huddled in cellars so long as fighting continued – two days or three at most – then they emerged to resume normal occupations. The Government must have known full well that this was madness, but it was powerless. By its irresolution – and example – it had set the ball rolling and it was helpless to stop it, especially among a people too prone to consider regulations as so much waste paper. From Bordeaux, whither the Cabinet had fled after a few days to Tours, Charles Pomaret, ephemeral Minister of the Interior, broadcast dramatically: "All inhabitants are ordered to remain where they are. The Government will see to it that this order is obeyed". King Canute could not stem the tide, neither could

16

Charles Pomaret. The emptiness of his words was all too evident. By this time Ministers and their orders were equally discredited.

Prior to this tardy manifestation of energy, the Government had rested content with "inviting" the people to refrain from joining the flight. But invitations imply that they may be declined. French individualism declined for the most part. Probably unequivocal orders would have been heeded, especially if they had come from the military. Why they never were given, or were given too late, surpasses understanding, for the endless flow on congested roads impeded movements of troops and jeopardized communications. The enemy, moreover, soon realised the advantages presented by this liquification of a whole nation. Its general staff took it into account with patent results. The flight of the civilian population helped to encompass the ruin of the Army.

Only long after the mad rush was there time to think of the flotsam and jetsam. Families and parties had become divided. Children had strayed and been lost. Reunion was a problem. For weeks the newspapers printed columns of personal announcements: "The wife of Charles Durand, of rue Manin, Paris, informs her husband that she is in safety in Perpignan". Or "Who can give news of Louise Dupont, of rue Neuve, Amiens? Write her mother, care of the Mayor of Toulouse". Those who had no money for advertisements chalked messages on the kerb as they passed by. One poor woman had been separated successively from each of her six children. Another, in the bombing of a train, had lost a six-month babe. A pathetic announcement at the end of July concerned a little girl "found in a wheat field" five weeks earlier. For months similar advertisements continued to appear. Even a year later a special organisation still strove to find the lost and strayed.

There were also the prisoners of war – nearly two million of them. How could they learn of the whereabouts of refugee relatives? Almost every family in the land had its domestic tragedy. Months afterwards some were awaiting news. Too often it took the form of word from a village priest: "Jules Martin was killed in the fighting here at the end of May". The rout was such that the Army could not keep track of its casualties.

But why was this exodus? Memories are short. They need refreshing. It was in the first days of September 1939 that France and Britain – the latter some hours before the former – notified Hitler's German Reich that they considered themselves at war because of the invasion of Poland. For eight months nothing of moment happened, beyond a minuet-like operation which took the French armies to the outworks of the Westwall and then brought them back to the outworks of the Maginot Line. People began to call it a "strange war", even a "funny war". In France and in Britain editors, and their readers after them, wondered why the Germans did nothing! "Why don't the silly fools advance? Time will tell against them. The blockade will bring them to terms."

On May 10 the Germans did advance. Within three days they had carved in the Allied lines a breach which never could be filled. By the end of the month they had won the Battle of Flanders. On June 5 began the Battle of France. On June 12 the Germans had won it. It had been revealed that on that date General Maxime Weygand, then Commander-in-Chief of what were still termed the Allied Armies, after presenting several pessimistic reports, proposed that an armistice should be requested. "The French Government demurred because public opinion was not sufficiently prepared." Next day the Germans entered Paris, forty-eight hours before the date set by their Führer. Fighting continued, but the war was over. The French defeat was complete. It marked the end of the Third Republic at the age of seventy years.

The military collapse was swift and startling. Yet it was nothing compared with the psychological symptom which accompanied it – that exodus of ten million souls; mad, yet understandable.

Later, when calm had returned, there was quibbling over figures. The desire was to reduce them. But Marshal Pétain himself had broadcast on June 25: "The exodus of refugees assumed unheard-of proportions. Ten million French, joining one and one-half million Belgians, precipitated themselves to the rear of our front in indescribable conditions of disorder and misery".

Why all this? The truth is that the war had become almost a joke, the inviolability of the Maginot Line a dogma. The French Cabinet headed by Edouard Daladier, the British Cabinet under Neville Chamberlain, had systematically minimised the scope of military operations. They iterated that there were to be "no rash offensives", which plain people took to mean that Hitler, at some time or other, would benevolently send his armies to be mown down by the Allies waiting behind their fortifications. Stress was laid on the very small number of casualties (scarcely more than one thousand, boasted Daladier after several months of hostilities), on the determination to husband human lives. Insignificant skirmishes between patrols in No Man's Land were magnified into important feats of arms; everything was done to induce the illusion that the war would ever continue thus. "This time," Ministers proclaimed, "the Fatherland is not open to invasion."

A few months later the Germans were nearing Bordeaux in the West, had reached Valence in the East! During all the preceding lull the chief concern had not been more men, more guns, more airplanes, but social centres at the front, footballs, books, card games, radio sets, "Daladier champagne" at Christmas, periodical furloughs and a generous distribution of medals. And reporters, pompously dubbed "war correspondents", were admitted into the army zone to glorify all this.

Truth to tell, there was discernible from the very first a potent reason for this coddling. The French had gone to war resigned but not enthusiastic. In the heart of every politician there lurked a dread of the soldiers thus brought into being by mobilisation – dread of their reactions, dread also of their eventual return as citizens once again, as voters also. Nothing was left undone that ingenuity could devise to induce them to believe that their fate was the prime concern of Government, Parliament and everyone in authority. There was even added to every staff in the field a branch known as G5 whose scope embraced press, radio, cinema, propaganda, social welfare, morale and publicity, and whose personnel was recruited largely among shirkers of all ranks, for the most part well provided with political pull.

Clear-sighted critics insisted that, like all wars, this one would be decided by the ordeal of battle and that battles mean killed, wounded and missing. Above all, they urged unceasing preparation. They deplored complacent inaction, pointed to its dangers, warned against its consequences. All to no purpose. In Paris, the leaders were too busy playing politics. Here it should be emphasised that under the late parliamentary regime in France the Government alone was responsible for the general conduct of the war, which definition comprises its military, diplomatic, economic, financial, industrial and political aspects, while the High Command was responsible only for the conduct of operations. This doctrine had been affirmed in a law on the organisation of the nation in time of war passed in 1938. Application of its details was still under consideration when hostilities began. Parliament, on its part, insisted on its prerogative of controlling the actions of Cabinet. As a consequence lobby intrigues never ceased. The game of politics continued in full swing.

Censorship aided in plunging the nation into a state of stupor, failing to awaken it to a sense of realities. And the Press remained supine under threat of suspension or suppression. In fact newspaper action proved lamentable. There was a general conspiracy tacitly to declare that everything was for the best in the best of all possible worlds, and to present the war as a newsreel filmed in very distant parts.

There was a high Commissioner for Information, it is true, eventually superseded by a full-fledged Cabinet Minister. But in each case the object seemed to be to stifle information rather than to impart it, as sufficiently symbolised by the fact that Information ruled over Censorship. The High Commissioner was Jean Giraudoux. Though animated by the best of intentions, he remained a novelist who had neither the experience nor the authority required for the task; nor was he free to choose his assistants. Swathed in red-tape, filled with protégés of influential politicians, his Commissariat was only one more bureaucratic stronghold in a land already stifled by bureaucracy.

Giraudoux could give no information because he had none. Callers at the Hôtel Continental – the largest in Paris, requisitioned for the Commissariat at great cost – were invariably pumped for news instead of it being given them. So that the Press, urged to present all things in the best light, descanted on the unlimited resources of the Allies, scoffed at German ration cards, magnified German railroad accidents (the Censor saw to it that no reports were printed of train wrecks in France) and generally contributed to creating a fool's paradise.

Information, propaganda and censorship were all housed in this Hôtel Continental. Huge though it was, it was never large enough for the swarm of shirkers and job seekers. Most of them were in uniform, drew Army pay, rode in Army automobiles, rattled imaginary sabres, browbeat civilians, cringed before politicians and, in sum, did nothing. Waiting one day in an antechamber for some subordinate official to return from lunch – it was then 3.30 pm – I was eyed with disdain by two young stenographers who soon resumed a conversation turning on dress, the movies and boyfriends. The sudden appearance of an officer scarcely disturbed them. To one of the girls he dictated about one hundred words and left with the indication: "Please type this immediately; it is urgent". The stenographer giggled and turned to her friend: "I didn't understand one word, did you?" Said the other: "I didn't even listen". In every room of the Continental there were secretaries such as these. Men or women, all clung to their sinecure like leeches. When the exodus came their automobiles were to be seen on every high road, claiming right of way.

Ludovic Oscar Frossard, a clever politician, who had tasted of Communism and abjured it, succeeded Giraudoux with the title of Minister. He inaugurated his tenure of office with a trip to London to meet his British counterpart and was there dined, wined and photographed. The purpose was to correlate the two services, but by that time the British Ministry of Information, with its notorious 999 employees, had become utterly discredited. Next Frossard took nearly one month to organise his Ministry. The list of his aides and advisers filled more than a column of the *Temps*. Of information there was still none.

But when the war did start Frossard got busy – with warnings calculated to strike terror in the heart of the people. Whether in communiqués or in broadcasts it was: "Beware of parachutists! Beware of the Fifth Column! Beware of the person next to you when you seek shelter during an air raid!" Beware of this, that and the other thing! And the newspapers were filled with stories of Dutch and Belgian refugees attacked from the air with bombs or machine-guns. All the talk was of atrocities. The Government had failed signally to make the French war-conscious; it succeeded only too well in making them terror-conscious. Hence the Great Exodus.

CHAPTER 2

HOW LITTLE THEY KNOW OF ENGLAND

Now the narrative can unfold in due order. It, also, opens with an exodus.

Every man has two countries, his own and France. So said Thomas Jefferson. For a Frenchman the second is either England or America – or both. That is my case. It was England at any rate that developed in me the concrete idea of liberty; in France it had remained abstract.

My quests into political philosophy, my vicarious exploration of America, have been made possible by three things – education by an old-time dominie, inability to learn shorthand, and introduction to a certain Mrs Peabody. The first proved the most important, for it gave me my first notions of liberalism.

When I was eight, circumstances led our family to migrate to England where I passed the next twelve years. I had been at a French lycée, with its dismal atmosphere (in those days schools in France were built like barracks or jails), its irksome discipline, its omnipresent ushers whether at study, at table, at play or in the dormitory, and its horror of fresh air and exercise. From this prison I was transplanted suddenly to a place where restrictions were implied rather than imposed, where trust was reposed even in a child's sense of honour. That impression of freedom marked my whole life.

Soon after our arrival in England my younger brother and myself were placed in the care of one Thomas Knight. He had a small boarding school at Hornsey, a suburb in the North of London, which then could still boast of trees and grass. The boys all belonged to the lower middle-class, destined to swell the ranks of obscure clerks and bookkeepers "in the city". It was quite modest but the very place to turn two young "Froggies" into English schoolboys. For three months we were allowed to run wild, picking up the vernacular by what is now styled the direct method. We roamed the fields, mixed in every crowd, hobnobbed with all and sundry and repeated slang and cuss-words with fluency.

Then Thomas Knight took our education in hand. He did not undertake to teach much, but to teach well. Above all, he made a point of teaching English, which was rather exceptional even at that period. In this regard I owe him a great debt. Knight was a true Victorian. Tall, portly, bearded like a Michelangelo Moses, garbed the year round in black Prince Albert and top hat, he oozed dignity, solidity, respectability. He must have been about sixty then. The boys called him Timmy, doubtless because his wife was Miggy.

The contrast could not have been greater. Miggy was the obvious name for her. Anyhow the school knew no other. Very short, very fat, apple-cheeked, quick of tongue yet motherly, she ruled over every domain but the classroom. She had borne Timmy five daughters. None had married. They helped their mother to care for some forty urchins, all the more unruly because well fed. But Miggy was up to all their tricks.

The house once had been what Victorians styled "a desirable residence for a gentleman", massive and drear. This particular gentleman must have fallen upon hard times and sold it cheap. Everything was tarnished and ill-repaired, but the rooms were vast and there was a large garden with paddock.

25

The paddock served as playground; Timmy took exercise tilling. He raised all the vegetables served at table. In addition each weekday he rose early to go to Smithfield Meat Market in the heart of London to buy the joint for dinner. He insisted on quality and it was cheaper there than in the village. He went by train, walking some two miles to the station. On the return journey two of the elder lads met him there, to carry the meat bags. The carriers went in turns and unanimously made out that it was a tiresome chore; yet they went with inward glee because of the opportunity to fill commissions for candy and marbles.

Miggy seldom left the house, yet she took exercise in her way. To all appearances she was always in the kitchen, where an ox could have been roasted whole on the spit. But nothing happened anywhere without her being there too. Preluding a raid on the apple barrel, scouts would report that Miggy was quietly darning socks. The raiders came in a rush – and nearly fell over Miggy! The woman's prescience was uncanny. Her invisible presence defended all her stores, from jam cupboard to larder.

Dinner was something of a ceremony, with unvarying ritual. Standing at the head of a long table, Timmy carved. Miggy at one side attended to the "two vegetables" of English tradition. Three of the daughters passed the plates. As his turn came, each boy sang out his preference: "Underdone, please Sir, no fat" or: "Well done, please Sir, with a little fat". Timmy cut generous portions. A boiled pudding invariably followed.

There was a ritual in the classroom also. The curriculum was limited to the three R's, grammar, some history and geography, a smattering of French, with shorthand as an extra. English was Timmy's favourite. He disdained text-books and always demonstrated at the blackboard. We boys used slates. For reading and dictation Timmy relied solely on the Bible and the editorial columns of *The Daily Telegraph*, the newspaper he received each day. The choice seems odd; possibly it was not deliberate; in reality it was excellent. It spanned the whole range of the language, for in those days the *Telegraph* was nothing if not "journalese". Its bright particular star was George Augustus Sala, who wrote "bifurcated garment" when he meant trousers and "hirsute appendage" when he meant whiskers. At one extreme we boys had the forthright prose of the Authorised Version, at the other a feast of pompous floridity. Although we were too young to discriminate between styles, good seed was then sowed.

Thomas Knight believed in instruction by rote. At the grammar hour the class stood round the room and conjugated verbs aloud, each in turn taking a tense. Se we reeled off; "Imperative mood: be, or be thou, or do thou be. Be, or be ye or you, or do ye or you be". Or, for the conditional: "I might, could, would or should be; thou mightst, couldst, wouldst or shouldst be, etc..." Educators may deplore the system as unintelligent, but its results endure – even after fifty years. In mathematics also Timmy had his own method. The favourite penalty in case of error was "a long multiplication", with thirty numerals in both multiplicand and multiplier, then proof by division.

On Sundays all went to church twice. Timmy was an Anglican, but tolerant. In the morning boys of other denominations went individually to their respective places of worship, but in the evening the whole school marched two by two to Hornsey Parish Church. It was very old, with tall pews that screened much silent mischief. The favourite places were near the wall, where during sermon you could dig deeply with a pocketknife into the crumbling beams. Afterwards, during supper – we filed past Miggy to receive a hunk of bread and cheese – scores of old magazines and picture-books were brought from a chest. Some dated far back, in particular an odd lot of the years 1863 and 1864, with many woodcuts of the Civil

War. To a young mind they gave an unsuspected aspect of America, quite stirring after *The Daily Telegraph*'s reports of Grover Cleveland's unending troubles over the tariff question. The next stage was to read Fenimore Cooper – and Buffalo Bill. And there awakened an interest in George Washington and Colonial days, then "From Log-Cabin to White House", as well as a confused perception of democracy.

In this setting the little "Froggies" thrived. It was all so different from the French lycée with its dismal atmosphere and its ambitious course of study, even in the lower grades. The French object seemed to be to turn out men-boys, while the English preferred boy-men. These were happy days at Hornsey, and profitable though we scarcely knew it. May Thomas Knight rest in peace – and Miggy also. Their disappeared long ago. Already in my time jerry-builders had taken the paddock. Today the "desirable residence for a gentleman" has given place to flats.

The only shadow in the picture was that many of the boys were Cockney and the "Froggies", knowing no better, had become Cockneys too. So after two years they were transferred to Bedford, to rid themselves of the accent and to imbibe that English public-school spirit which wins Waterloo, turns out Oxford and Cambridge dons, civil servants, generals, admirals, bishops, statesmen and viceroys – or merely country squires and remittance men. It may have its drawbacks in that it tends to perpetuate obsolescent traditions, but on the other hand it forms character and develops esprit de corps. Many things have changed in fifty years, it is true, but the English public-school remains definitely English, even after two wars.

Materially there were many contrasts between the French and English systems of education; morally there was this in particular: in France everything was regulated and circumscribed and one's movements were watched all the time;

in England there was complete liberty, checked only by the unwritten law of those things which simply are not done. When they were done, the chastisement was accepted stoically, whether birching or caning.

All this, however, was singular preparation for a life destined to be intimately linked with America and Americans. As a matter of fact the question of a career seemed rather hazy then. Dislikes were clear; likes less so. Business was not congenial; ways and means precluded consideration of any liberal profession. So one fine day I was articled to the editor of the *Bedfordshire Times & Independent*, one of the four weekly newspapers of which the town then boasted. It was Liberal in politics and reported local events exhaustively; soon it absorbed one of the rival sheets and appeared twice a week. The "articles of apprenticeship" covered a period of four years; the first unpaid, the others with nominal salary – bare pocket-money. In due legal form the editor contracted to teach the apprentice his trade; the apprentice, on his part, was pledged by parent or guardian to be diligent and obedient. The custom was to call the apprentice an "articled pupil"; it sounded more genteel.

In practice, the "articled pupil" taught himself by tackling all the chores of a small town paper. There was much to say for the system. A keen lad could learn much in four years, familiarising himself with the routine of every department, from type-setting and proof-reading to reporting and general writing, including advertising copy. The young reporter roamed the countryside on a bicycle, attending meetings of rural bodies and police court sessions, recording births, marriages and deaths, harvest festivals, cattle sales and what not, and generally picking up unconsidered trifles.

It was a tribute to the teaching of Thomas Knight that a French youth was able to hold his own among English reporters; it was a tribute to the apprenticeship system that he was able later to qualify as a regular American newspaper man. Bedford, in point of fact, was an excellent centre for such early training. It was sufficiently near the Metropolis to escape utter provincialism. With education as its chief trade (a Bedford boy who had become Lord Mayor of London had endowed numerous schools), it could pride itself on a measure of culture. Attracted by these schools, many residents came with their families from India and the colonies, mostly retired officers or civil servants, with the result that, in the aggregate, the outlook was much broader than in most market towns.

Moreover Bedford cherished the memory of two celebrities, John Bunyan of *Pilgrim's Progress*, and John Howard, of prison reform fame. Bunyan in particular continued to be a source of inspiration, a symbol of freedom of thought and of rebellion against tyrannical conformity. The environment was favourable to the development of a young mind which in France had been imbued early with the spirit of the Revolution and which was beginning to inquire into political systems. So in this middle-class town we bought the *Clarion* by stealth and imbibed dear old Robert Blatchford's brand of Socialism, forceful but tolerant. William T. Stead was another influence, sincere but reasoning from very personal axioms. A master journalist, he yet retained a degree of naivety which had its charm. It was he who during the siege of Paris in 1870-71 roasted mice on the office fire – he was then with the *Darlington Echo* – and ate them on toast, "to write with knowledge" of the privations of the Parisians forced to consume rats.

America was still very distant. In those days it was virtually an unknown land to an English country town. When the *Times & Independent*, to celebrate its fiftieth anniversary, ventured to seek greetings from editors of papers published in all the Bedfords and New Bedfords of the United States, it was almost like sending a message to Mars. But the replies served to impress one American trait – hospitality to the stranger and cheerful readiness to be of service. The Spanish-American War, on the other hand, cast a shadow.

At that time America was known to the average Englishman chiefly through her humorists, Mark Twain, Artemus Ward, Josh Billings, who, judging by the many extracts printed in the popular weeklies, typified American thought and American ways. Their style and their spelling struck the fancy because so uncouth and led more than one to imagine that everyone spoke that way in that strange land. Fortunately, successive acquaintance with Lowell, Hawthorne, Longfellow, Irving, Poe, Holmes, Emerson even, served to restore the balance.

Nevertheless the vision of America continued dim – a jumble of bearded Union generals, ringleted Southern cavaliers, tobacco-chewing Yankees, black-face minstrels, pirating publishers, dollar-seeking traders and Puritanical reformers, against a background of Red Indians, Negroes, Chinese, gold-diggers, oil prospectors, cowboys – and Blondin crossing Niagara Falls. But all very distant, very unreal, and it must be confessed more amusing than serious. That image persisted for four years during which the budding reporter returned to France to become a conscript.

In my native land every youth was inured to the idea of conscription, to serving in the Army on reaching man's estate. It was part of current life. All thought of a career was conditioned by the phrase "after my military service". And the progression was accepted: Boy, Soldier, Man. It was hard, but it was the law.

England, still completely insular, had no conception of conscription. She has learned since, this among many things. She was changing already when, freed from service, I returned periodically. My recollections of late Victorian days were of a land of freedom. True, Mrs Grundy imposed her will and Sunday was the dismal height of boredom. But the Englishman's home was still his castle, bureaucracy was discreet and so long as a citizen was law-abiding he could do what he pleased, in his pursuit of happiness. Gladstonian Liberalism may not have been democratic in the sense now given to the word; it was too prone to imagine that parliamentary government had inherent virtues which could transform at one stroke cannibal savages into an enlightened community. But it stood for a wide measure of individual freedom and tolerance without which I, for one, cannot conceive democracy.

The First World War encroached on civil liberties in England as elsewhere and the encroachments persisted when peace returned. The State, in the person of its bureaucrats, began to poke its nose into the Englishman's castle; Gladstonian Liberals must have turned in their graves when the Postmaster-General was given authority to open the Englishman's letters, lest they contain tickets for the Irish Sweepstake. Questionnaires to be filled, information to be given, prohibitions of all kinds, and a multiplication of boards, authorities and commissions, some with semi-judicial powers – such was England just prior to this war. The late Lord Banbury, a typical Victorian, devoted his parliamentary career to endeavour to stem the ever increasing flow of restrictive legislation. But what could he do single-handed?

Yet England retained – and still retains despite another war – some sound fundamentals of liberty and democracy. One of them is: "What the soldier said is not evidence". As prentice reporter it was part of my duties to attend courts, both civil and criminal. There I learned one thing, which I was then too callow to appreciate but which experience has now thrown into relief. Britons may not realise it because they accept it as a matter of course, but they should understand that their Law of Evidence equals in importance most other institutions, even including Magna Carta and the Habeas Corpus Act. It is the very foundation of the British Empire; nay, it is a factor in the formation of the British character. Fair evidence implies fair play, whether in a court of law or on the cricket field. Testimony on oath, at first-hand, in public and with faculty to cross-examine, should be regarded as Britain's most cherished possession.

If one entered a court in France, in Italy, in any other country of Europe, even in pre-authoritarian days, the contrast with British methods appalled. Criminal trials might be public, but their preparation was secret. For years in France the accused was not even allowed the aid of a lawyer when questioned by an examining magistrate; this was the rule also in several other countries. That magistrate had virtually unlimited powers. He might leave the accused in jail for months, even years before sending the case for trial or signing his release because of insufficient proof. At the trial the judge questioned not only the accused but the witnesses also, and the latter might say what they pleased, how they pleased. They might say: "I know nothing of the facts, but I was told by a friend, who had it from a neighbour, that everyone believes the accused is the sort who would steal a penny from a blind man". And there was no one to interpose: "What the soldier said is not evidence".

With defeat things went from bad to worse. France became authoritarian. Law was replaced by laws, ever limitative in effect. Some were retroactive, others mortgaged the future; they confiscated possessions "present and to come". And there was invented that derision "administrative justice", whereby officialdom could intern and impound by a stroke of the pen.

Britain also stood alone in Europe as a country where officials might be held responsible – and penalised – for their actions; damages might even be obtained by suing the police. Everywhere else, including France, bureaucrats enjoyed complete immunity for acts "in the exercise of their functions". Nor, before the war, were Britons subjected to many inquisitions, although the thin end of the edge had been driven in. In France if I wished to enter my son in a Government school – for the Army, Navy, Colonial Service, for instance – a policeman would come to my home and ask such impertinent questions as: "What are your means?" Or "What are your political affiliations?" And the answers would be filed in a "dossier" to be consulted so long as I and my son lived. Lucky Britons who had no "dossiers" unless they had criminal records, and even then those records were produced only after conviction.

Nevertheless – and in spite of the Law of Evidence – Britain is a paradox and likely to remain so; a country with an aristocratic constitution veiled by democratic leanings, the whole held together by sentimental traditions and a strongly developed civic sense. For that reason and regardless of externals, Britain ever was more democratic in spirit than France. British liberties, under an aristocratic oligarchy, could have been a model for the world.

It was all paradoxically anti-democratic, yet that very oligarchy, whether by right of birth or by wealth, felt as a whole constrained to serve. It might be ostentatious, even after death – "Remember St. Dunstan's in your will!" ran appeals for funds for the institution of blind soldiers – but it was accepted as a civic duty. For years in England hospitals, life-boats, lighthouses, homes for the common herd as well as for "needy gentlewomen", charities by the score, were "supported by voluntary contributions". It was an illogical system, possibly immoral, but it stood the test. "John Bull, scratching his head, but still subscribing!" And his testamentary benevolence was printed in the public sheets!

Yet, whatever she was, whatever she may be, Britain is likely to remain difficult to understand. Neither has she ever understood others easily. Insularity tells. This mutual difficulty of comprehension had its effect on Anglo-French relations, even in the heyday of the Entente Cordiale. In this war the misunderstanding reached its highest point. There has been much bitterness, which each side may justify to its satisfaction. It may pass. It all depends on the turn of events.

Certainly the British were ill prepared for a test of arms, but the French were no less so. And, after all, the general direction of operations, as well as the doctrine of war, had been left to the French. All the emphasis moreover was on defence, with the Maginot Line a symbol for both. The British understood it in their own way, and that may serve in a measure to explain why they sent so few troops to France. The French argue that when the crisis came their allies might have given greater help. But at that time it was clear already that defeat was probable, if not inevitable. General Maxime Weygand held out little hope after the Battle of Flanders.

The French argue also that for many years their diplomacy followed in the wake of Britain. This is manifest. But France was a sovereign State and mistress of her own policies. The British could retort fairly that they were not responsible for the supineness of the French leaders. Certainly for many years they took advantage of such weakness; then, at the crucial moment, they deluded themselves into believing that these leaders were strong, strong enough at least to galvanise the people to further resistance. In reality France was whipped, worse whipped than any nation ever was. The description is Pétain's.

France in her masses was apathetic. These masses never knew exactly why war had been declared, they never knew how it was being fought, and it took months before they realised not only the extent of the defeat but its full meaning. The demeanour of the crowds at Bordeaux in June 1940 was eloquent in this regard.

The invader was advancing fast – to the very gates of the city. Yet even this prospect could not shake apathy. There were individual exceptions – the four-star Admiral so dejected as he walked the street, that Air Force captain so deep in reflection in a restaurant that he sent back his plate untouched, that grandmother weeping and sobbing, as she clasped a child to her bosom. But the mass continued to live its daily life, waiting dully. And when the Germans did enter Bordeaux, that mass lined the avenues to watch the parade, open-mouthed and wide-eyed, still apparently unmoved, though here and there teeth gritted and eyes dimmed. Circus had come to town. The reason for all this may be discerned later.

It was then held by some, and these cling to their belief, that it would have been preferable to continue the struggle, directed from North Africa or London, or even from some possession in America. Possibly something might have been done. The fleet was still in being, but it would have been no easy matter to transport troops, and the Air Force was reduced to nothing; at best there were airplanes, but no landing fields, no ground crews, no supplies. It was not a matter of fighting force but of national morale. And that morale was ebbing fast in the general apathy. However much it might strike men still fighting as sacrilegious, the news of the armistice was received with relief by the mass. Not that it understood what it meant, but simply because it marked the end of the war and of the exodus. And at dusk, in the streets of Bordeaux, there began to lurk soldiers in uniform, stragglers from whom one recoiled instinctively.

Against the British the French long held two things. The first was that in May 1940 they did not respond to

Weygand's call to strive to fill the breach between Bapaume and Péronne. On May 23 that breach had been reduced from thirty miles to about fifteen; the next day the British forces changed their line of march and proceeded North-West, in the direction of Dunkirk – and home (it was said in bitterness "never put the British soldiers near the sea, the temptation to embark is too strong"). In consequence the hope vanished of stemming the flood of German tanks. Then came the Belgian surrender. Such is the French case. Until the British, Belgian and German reports on this tragic phase are available, impartial history can scarcely be written. But soon some first impressions were modified.

This was notably so as regards the Belgians. It is averred now that their King was no "felon", that his army fought valiantly until it would have been madness to continue, and that there was no blotch on the national escutcheon. Nor were the British without champions. French politicians nurtured on opportunism - and some ambitious officers, admirals even, must be reckoned among them – thought that it would serve their ends to belittle British effort and to speak of Dunkirk as a shame. Just as Paul Reynaud had heaped contumely upon Leopold so François Darlan, who had fawned to revive for himself the rank of admiral of the fleet, spat venom on Britain. When hell was let loose at Dunkirk he was safe ashore, as were also those subordinates who later thrived on their sycophancy until ousted in their turn by Pierre Laval's Thurifers, whose name was legion.

Yet even in this period, when greed vied with servility, and intolerance reigned supreme, some voices rose to proclaim historic truth. Darlan, for instance never forgave Benoit Léon de Fornel de La Laurencie both for this patrician enumeration of names and for a letter, widely circulated, in which he told the true story of Dunkirk. That general had commanded an army corps there and wrote of what he knew, indignant and forthright.

He had added to his sins dignified opposition to the Germans as delegate of the Vichy government in Paris. Yet Darlan dared not order his arrest. Laval dared.

The second charge against the British related to the attack on French warships at Mers-el-Kébir in July 1940. The French insist that from the very moment it was deemed not only necessary but imperative to ask for a cessation of hostilities, one of their chief concerns was to assure that their fleet would not be used against their late allies. They assert that in Bordeaux the British Ambassador was informed of this determination repeatedly. They add that the terms of the armistice would have been easier but for this. Consequently they describe the firing on ships at their moorings as cold-blooded murder of more than two thousand men.

The fact is inescapable on the other hand that Paul Reynaud, as Prime Minister, had pledged France not to sign a separate peace. History will judge all this. Pétain once – in 1940 when he was still lucid – said: "I do not accuse England. Every country has a right to act as it considers best for its own defence".

One great fault of the British was to imagine that certain French leaders really led. One great fault of the French was to imagine that throughout the world France was loved for herself. They still believed that love of France was a matter of course and they dwelt on such phrases as "vanguard of civilisation" and "bearer of the torch of liberty". But they did nothing to foster that love or to retain it.

Take, for example, Paul Reynaud's eleventh-hour appeal to the United States. It was pathetic, heart-rending; it was so manifestly useless. Why should America enter the war? How could she at that time? A few days later, when all was over, Jean Prouvost, the publisher, appeared once again in the part of High

Commissioner for Information. One of his underlings, arrogant and jaunty in his lieutenant's uniform, received American correspondents in his name. His greeting was: "Can you explain why our man in New York consistently urged us to declare war, on the plea that America would join?" None deigned answer. The question merely proved that France still knew little of America.

I have given my native country one-eighth of my life as a soldier in peace and war, and Army service has left its mark on my philosophy. Even a private second class may think usefully.

CHAPTER 3

YOU'RE A SOLDIER NOW

Life as a conscript in France came as a great shock to a youth raised in England. From the first day all accepted values were reversed. Individuality was checked at its very blossoming; it had to fight hard for survival. Three years of such existence was an ordeal from which most emerged either tempered or dulled, save the vegetative. That was forty years ago. Many things have changed and two wars have intervened, yet the fundamentals remain the same.

Here was a young man in whose previous life any restraints had been justified by reason: duty to one's self, to one's fellows. "Liberty, Equality, Fraternity" had been the appeal, even though representing then only an abstract formula. The concept of democracy had become synonymous with the idea of freedom. Suddenly all freedom ceased, whether of mind or body. The individual was lost in the mass and man became a machine, moving at the bidding of other machines ranking superior simply because they wore stripes. Unquestioning conformity was imposed by Regulations. And periodically there was read out that marrow-freezing document, the Code of Military Justice, with its inhuman iteration of penalties: death, death, death, or at the least forced labour for life, with the invariable prelude of "military degradation".

Today America has conscription; the lessons apply to her henceforth. That these were not empty formulas was soon made evident. The process of "military degradation" occurs in

France at what is known as an "execution parade". Within a month we recruits witnessed one. An artillery corporal had committed a rather serious offense. So far as I can recall he had led in free hours a rather gay life beyond his means; one day he sought to obtain money by threats. Normally that would be a common-law matter, but in France in those days a soldier was invariably court-martialled whatever the charge. Possibly the man had used a pistol, seeing that for some weeks the talk of the garrison turned on firing squads, each conscript recoiling from the idea that it might be his turn of duty.

The boy was sentenced for life and early one chilly December morn all the recruits were marched to the artillery barracks to attend the "execution parade". In a long life I have no recollection of anything so gloomy, more forbidding. Everything was sombre. The entire artillery regiment was there, in the black uniform of those days. It formed three sides of a square; infantry recruits in steel-grey greatcoats made the fourth. All was hushed. Then there drove up a penitentiary wagon from which emerged a lone figure – the convict. Immediately surrounded by a guard with drawn sabre, he was led to the centre of the square, bareheaded. "In the name of the French People", an officer read the sentence, ending with the words "military degradation". Whereupon a sergeant ripped off the corporal's stripes, his brass buttons and red facings and piping's, all lightly stitched in advance – and with dramatic gesture cast them to the ground. The convict, a tall, handsome lad, stood out a ghastly figure, all black save for the livid face. Then he was marched along the four sides of the square, back to the wagon – a hearse for a living man. It was one way of telling each recruit there: "My boy, you're in the Army now!"

It impressed me all the more since, as military age approached, there had been some searching of heart. What was the proper course? The easy one was to remain in England, eventually to become a subject of Her Most Gracious Majesty the Widow of Windsor. But that would have entailed exclusion from France until the age of forty-five; under French law acquisition of British nationality did not remove military obligations. I decided to pay the "blood tax" and on a bleak November day, thirty six hours after leaving London, I found myself in an infantry barrack room at Nancy, then a frontier garrison, ruefully contemplating a jumble of clothing and equipment tumbled on a narrow bed, my sole belongings for the next three years.

It was hard, in every way. Much progress has been made, but even today, despite Pétain's would-be patriarchal regime, barracks can scarcely be held up as models of cheeriness or cleanliness. And Army mentality ran in a singular groove. Every three months, for instance, there was a bed-bug hunt. All bedding was turned out into the yard and there was much splashing of kerosene and burning of sulphur. But the efforts were limited to extermination, never to prevention. In those days, too, the moral welfare of the soldier was scarcely considered. Other than the canteen there was no place for relaxation. The barrack-room, ill-lit, ill-heated, served every purpose; there the men slept, dressed, cleaned their uniform and equipment, read, wrote, smoked. Prior to my service they ate there also; the provision of refectories had been considered a revolutionary innovation. Much of our time was passed alternately soiling and cleaning the barrack-room. Over the plumbing it is charitable to draw a veil.

We rose early of course and duty ended nominally at 5 pm with roll-call at nine and lights out an hour later. For four hours we were free to leave the barracks; but the evening meal was served at five also and, in any case, before going into town one had to change from fatigue overalls into uniform and satisfy the inspection of the sergeant at the gate. In practice moreover places of recreation were restricted to cafes, especially in winter; in the street you were saluting superiors at every step, for Nancy had an important garrison. The poor fellow dependent on Army pay at one cent a day seldom left barracks. Social centres for soldiers were in their infancy, under Catholic auspices. And in those days Republicanism rather frowned upon such Church initiative.

Nancy was headquarters for the Iron Division, the crack corps of the French Army, destined in case of war to hold key positions on the frontier while the rear mobilised. Consequently recruits were trained intensively; within three months they had to be ready to take to the field. For those three months it was everlasting drill, drill, drill. Barrack-yards being too small, squads went out into the fields or mustered on the Cours Leopold, Nancy's vast promenade, there to be bawled at by the drill-sergeant to the great delight of grinning urchins and giggling nursemaids. It was exceedingly monotonous and not a little humiliating.

Once the recruits were fit for war service, they went further afield for exercises and manoeuvres and it was more interesting, despite the rather ominous realisation that we were treading future battlefields on which possibly many of us were destined to fall. We were famed for our marching. Physically we were kept very fit and benefited much by outdoor life. And by dint of being told that we were fine fellows we came to believe it and were inordinately proud of ourselves. They call it "esprit de corps"; at bottom it is mere vanity.

One summer morn a bugle call would turn us out at three o'clock, grousing. The early mist heralded a sweltering day. Still grousing, we would march fifteen miles, not a few cross-country, potted with blank cartridges at dragoons from Pont-à-Mousson, then back to Nancy, sweating and panting, all in, cursing the life, yearning only for the hard bed on which to fall and lie inanimate for hours.

But on the Place Stanislas the general was waiting to take the salute. The band blared a quick march. And grousing no more we threw out our chests, raised our chins and stepped briskly past the admiring citizenry as if to say: "You may well look at us, good people. We're the boys of the Iron Division!"

Forty years later that esprit de corps was still there, despite months in the trenches, many times over the top, and heavy losses. A battalion came down from the lines, worn and wan, unkempt and filthy, with ranks woefully reduced. And all grousing. The men had but one thought – rest, on the bare earth if need be.

The word passed along that the general would take the salute. Tortured flesh rebelled at the notion and muttered oaths rose from the column, with not a top sergeant to dare expostulate. But at the first note of the waiting band it was the old story – chests thrown out, chins raised, brisk stepping past a crowd of villagers and spick-and-span shirkers, as if to say: "We're frowsy and lousy, and we stink. Corpses are rotting up there. But if it weren't for the likes of us what in Hell would happen to the like of you. Yes, look at us well! We're the boys of the Iron Division!"

But we little cared that we were destined to become heroes and service was a sore trial morally and mentally, the very negation of those democratic ideals which it was the duty of the Army to defend. Liberty went by the board. One was prepared for that. But equality? In its incidence the "blood tax" weighed very unevenly, far from universal in application. Some served three years, others but one. And class distinctions were not absent.

For a time after the reverses of the Franco-Prussian War of 1870-71 conscripts had served five years, with a system of drawing lots under which the lucky ones were released at the end of twelve months. Moreover certain exemptions were provided, favouring various professions "useful to the State", notably teachers and students of diverse kinds. And over and above this, young men could "volunteer conditionally" for one year if they pledged themselves to become Reserve officers and paid for their equipment and maintenance while under the colours.

Nothing could have been more contrary to the notion of equality of burden. In practice exempts and volunteers were all of one social class. On what career could a man launch after five years in the Army? An endeavour to remedy this flagrant injustice was made in 1889, when the term was reduced to three years and "voluntariat" was abolished. But exemptions were maintained. To make them more palatable in a democracy they were extended to men supporting families, to sons of widows, to those with a brother already in the Army. But in the main they favoured the same class as before – those preparing for the liberal professions. There was much abuse. A flagrant example was provided by the School of Oriental Language; a mere pass in Arabic or Persian saved the student two years of service. Having been educated in England, with no French degree or diplomas, I had to go through the mill – three years with "the common people". Twice we saw some of our fellows released before we could return home. At the end of the first twelvemonth I was promoted corporal, at the end of the second, sergeant.

Certainly the Army is the hardest of schools and too often its influence is evil. It is no place for weaklings, physical or moral. Some such gave up the struggle early, deserted and fled abroad, there to await periodical amnesties. I knew of two such in particular. They regretted it later and had trouble to live it down. Nevertheless one, Henri Bernstein, became a successful playwright – and an émigré in America in 1940 – while the other ended as managing editor of a Paris newspaper.

45

To those of sterner stuff Army life taught something invaluable: to know men and how to handle them. From that angle I can say honestly today that I do not regret those three years, heavy handicap though they proved.

From the very first the promiscuity was a trial for the squeamish. The bed next to mine was occupied by a man who had arrived so drunk, that it took him three days to recover. When addressed he would struggle to his feet, introduce himself in the hoarsest of voices as: "Jean Koch, coal-heaver from Grenelle" (a Paris slum) and fall back on his bed. Yet Jean Koch proved to be a sterling fellow, tough and coarse but with a heart of gold.

There were some much worse. They revealed themselves the first Sunday we recruits were allowed out of barracks, shepherded by "ancients", men in their second or third year. Tradition ordained that on those occasions we should make the round of the city's cheapest dives, frequented by the lowest class of prostitutes, those significantly known as "soldiers' women" – a strange initiation for the majority.

The pity of it was that this "gay life" was not without its lure for simple lads. Revisiting Nancy years later, I met in the street a man who had been sergeant with me. The father was a prosperous farmer, but the son had never returned to the plough. Country routine was too dull after a taste of the city. He was peddling coffee from door to door; his seedy looks told their tale.

There were other tragedies. "Poor Chicago" for instance. No one ever called him by his real name. He had lived some years in the Middle West of the United States; hence his sobriquet. Almost toothless, low-witted, he mumbled an unintelligible mixture of French and unassimilated American. Some corporals and sergeants, too prone to become petty tyrants, interpreted this as back-talk. So inoffensive "Chicago" was always in trouble. Minor offense piled upon minor offense and his record of misdemeanours grew ever longer. Seldom released from the guard-house, he was still serving out his time when we were discharged, for in those days terms in jug did not count as service. Heaven only knows how long he remained, lucky at that not to have been transferred to a labour battalion in Africa.

During the whole of those three years "Chicago" was my only contact with America, apart from an abortive attempt to impress my platoon with my American connections as well as my linguistic abilities. That was in 1900 when the autumn army manoeuvres were held in the neighbourhood of Rheims in the presence of His Majesty the Tsar of All the Russias. It rained eighteen days on end so that at the finish we stank like so many wet dogs. One morning while at rest by the roadside we noted the approach of the Minister of War, attended by all the foreign military attachés. He of the United States was my mark. The intention was to step out and greet him in my best American. As the cavalcade came near I prepared my little speech. Then I sallied forth, only to receive such a splash of muddy water from his horse's hoofs that I sputtered for several minutes while he rode by. The incident turned to my confusion but in later years it served as repeated introduction to T. Bentley Mott, long military observer in France for the Washington Administration. For the rest America remained a very distant land.

The curse of such a life was that it tended to numb the mental faculties in the never-ending succession of drill and fatigue. When there was any leisure, the appeal was all to the material appetites. Our officers were competent in their profession and generally well-meaning, but they remained a caste apart. Louis Hubert Gonzalve Lyautey, then a junior cavalry officer, destined to become a great colonial administrator and a Marshal of France, had not yet written for

47

the *Revue des Deux Mondes* that article on "The Social Role of the Officer" which marked an epoch in the evolution of military thought in France. In those days the Army was still distant from the Nation.

I am dwelling on this subject because of its bearing, not only on the history of France but on that of Europe and of Democracy in general; it serves also to explain certain aspects of the World War of 1914-18 and it should not be overlooked today. All this, of course, was borne upon my mind later. During my three years of service there was scant opportunity for study, even for reflection; yet the observations then made are essential to a complete picture of the times.

France was emerging from the throes of the Dreyfus Affair, which not only split the country in twain but several times threatened the existence of the regime itself. The Dreyfus Affair cannot be understood without a survey of the background. Since the Revolution of 1789 France had passed through a succession of political upheavals after each of which power remained with the regime which enjoyed the support of the Army. Napoleon is a case in point. The main concern of governments therefore was to remove the Army from politics. Thus the Third Republic, in its turn, disfranchised the military; neither officers nor soldiers could vote. The Army became known as "La Grande Muette" – the Great Silent One. But this very severance from national life defeated the purpose of the civil authority; it welded the Army into a class apart, which developed its own philosophy, its own traditions. By "Army" is meant here primarily the corps of officers, but the dogma of blind obedience, in the name of discipline, practically determined the attitude of the rank and file. The Army had its own regulations, its own code of honour, its own set of laws, its own courts, its own rules for promotion. So that, with a wave of anti-Semitic feeling aiding, it was possible to convict of treason

Captain Alfred Dreyfus and to resist for twelve years all efforts to prove his innocence.

Similar conditions then obtained in all European countries with large standing armies, though they might originate from different situations. In Imperial Germany and Imperial Austria the corps of officers was virtually above the law. In other States the Army – or the Navy – overthrew the regime periodically, as in Spain, Portugal, and Serbia. A Pretorian guard has always been a menace to its master.

In France the outcome of the Dreyfus Affair was to subordinate more and more the military authority to the civil. For instance, one of the first acts of Georges Clemenceau – he had been one of the stoutest defenders of Dreyfus – on coming to power in 1906 was to modify a Napoleonic decree which at every rung of the ladder gave Army officers precedence over civilian officials. There was a general endeavour to democratize the Army. But this also, in the very nature of things, had an inherent defect – it introduced the political factor into an organisation from which it was desired to exclude it. Opinions and beliefs came to play their part in determining promotion. The caste spirit was shattered, which was a gain, but it was replaced by a political criterion, which was a danger.

It was only human therefore that some ambitious officers should be tempted to become "yes-men" and, for motives of expediency, to accept certain military doctrines of the value of which they might be dubious. Thus objective students of the First World War are inclined to ascribe to the new trend of thought those early reverses, such as the loss of the Battle of the Frontiers, which proved so costly in men as well as in territory. In truth the process had begun some years before the Dreyfus Affair, which served merely to intensify it. This mentality had not disappeared by the time of the First World War and it was discernible even in the second.

CHAPTER 4

DOCTRINES COST LIVES

In those Nancy days, I was much too young in years, a mere novice in things military, to have any real knowledge of such matters, let alone a personal opinion. Yet I was privileged to meet there men who later played a prominent part either in the First World War or its preliminaries. Not that a mere sergeant normally mixes with the great, but I was fortunate enough to be introduced to social circles they frequented. I profited by their conversations. Three stand out: Victor Constant Michel, Audemard d'Alençon and Edouard de Curières de Castelnau. But their parts cannot be understood without first considering the background. Which, incidentally, may have a bearing on the peace, which is to follow the Second World War.

Governments always need money, democratic governments most of all for their social and other reforms. Increased taxation is ever unpopular; retrenchment in expenditure for defence is tempting. Moreover, pacific pronouncements have the ear of the masses. The Army may have doubts about the wisdom of such retrenchment, but if the Government insists it is prone to become opportunist and to seek to justify its attitude by evolving a new war doctrine to fit.

Specifically, after the reverses of 1870-71, French policy was concentrated upon defence and reliance on permanent fortifications. The idea was to strengthen both the Eastern frontier, facing Germany, and the Northern frontier, facing Belgium; so that the aggressor would be compelled either to seek passage through certain predetermined gaps behind which field armies could be massed to meet him, or to resort to siege operations. In this concept as much importance was attached to the Northern border as to the Eastern, since the shortest road from Cologne and Aachen to Paris is through Belgium, then down the valley of the Oise. Many times in French history has an invader taken this route. It was not overlooked in 1914 and 1940.

This system of defence was logic itself. After the fall of Napoleon in 1815 the Coalition gave France a frontier based on strategic considerations. The object was to prevent French armies from overrunning Europe again and, conversely, to facilitate operations by foreign armies on French soil. These considerations were emphasised in the Treaty of Frankfurt 1871. For a generation thereafter the French accepted the defensive as the course dictated by circumstances. An engineer of genius, General Séré de Rivières, devised the system of forts and gaps, while Field Regulations recommended caution in engaging action, with reliance on counter-attacks.

But by 1900 a change had come, under the gradual and conjoined influence of a number of factors. Fortification had proved a heavy burden on budgets as well as irksome to progressive communities; for example Lille, heart of the textile industry, which wanted to expand more and more. In the "eighties" the venture of General Georges Boulanger to become dictator had produced a twofold effect – it had reawakened the hope of those who wanted to recover Alsace and Lorraine by force of arms, and it had revived the fear, latent since Bonaparte, of a coup d'état by a popular commander. The Dreyfus Affair soon thereafter had sapped confidence in the Second Bureau (Army Intelligence Service). The War College, of recent creation, had adopted the Napoleonic campaigns as the basis of its teaching. The conviction persisted that war would continue to be waged solely by standing armies.

By the interplay of these and other factors there developed a new doctrine which gave pride of place to the offensive. It was argued that the ultimate victor is he who immediately imposes his will on the enemy, that the only way to compel that enemy to show his hand is to attack him, that the national temperament demanded a return to the "furia francesa" which had won so many victories in the past, and that in war offensive action alone, at all points and at all times, can bring a decisive result. The upshot was that Field Regulations were revised. When the new version was issued in October 1913 it condemned caution as pusillanimous and accepted unreservedly "l'offensive à outrance". It did not seek to conceal the fact that the doctrine implied "bloody sacrifices". But there was one omission of appalling significance – there was not a mention of machine-guns!

This new doctrine was welcomed by most of those faced by thorny problems; it provided easy solutions. Budgets could be relieved of appropriations for fortifications now denounced as hampering bold action. Training camps for the Reserve became unnecessary, since the offensive called primarily for Regulars. The expense of heavy field artillery could be saved, since the "75" was considered the ideal gun for attack. The Second Bureau could not hope to regain its pre-Dreyfus power, since the new Regulations went so far as to reprove delay in action for lack of information.

Above all the doctrine satisfied those political circles haunted by the dread of a military coup d'état. Their fears were stilled by Article 7 of the Regulations: "In view of the enormous size of the masses now brought into the field, the general battle will be the sum of the battles fought by individual armies, more or less distinct one from the other, but linked by a general concept". In plain words this meant that there was no longer need of a commander-in-chief. From a responsible supreme leader, authority was transferred to irresponsible lieutenants. The conduct of operations passed from generals to their anonymous staffs. Now that strategy and tactics had been reduced to their simplest expression – attacking the enemy as soon as sighted – loyalty to the regime, or more correctly to the Cabinet of the day, could be made the criterion for promotion to the highest ranks. So patent did this trend become that the Army soon realised that a career depended as much on acceptance of the new doctrine as on professional skill.

One of the most active apostles of the new school of thought had been a mere subaltern, Captain Gilbert, in many ways an earlier counterpart of Britain's Captain B.H. Liddell Hart, whose theories have been accepted as having inspired Leslie Hore-Belisha during his iconoclastic term at the War Office in London. Gilbert had a great mind in a frail body. Stricken by paralysis, he propagated from a sick-bed views which found ready approval in many quarters. Some years later upon the creation of the Centre for Higher Military Studies, known familiarly in the Army as "the Field Marshal's School", these views were supported with vigour by one of the lecturers, Colonel de Grandmaison, who also acquired considerable influence.

Some few officers of the old school strove to demonstrate the fallacy of the doctrine, but Gilbert and Grandmaison won the day. One of the unbelievers was Philippe Pétain. In 1914 he was still a colonel of infantry, within a few months of retirement given his age. He was noted for his independent views; his confidential record bore the marginal indication: "Never to be promoted general". When the new doctrine was elaborated in his presence he would reply in two words: "Fire kills". A few years later Philippe Pétain, the man who was never to be promoted, was Commander-in-Chief,

Victor of Verdun, Marshal of France – and twenty years afterwards Chief of State at the patriarchal age of eighty-four!

Again after the Treaty of Versailles politics played their part in shaping a military doctrine. Victory had been bought at a heavy price – 1 500 000 French dead. And repeatedly it had been snatched from defeat – twice on the Marne, once at Verdun. Literally France was blinded by that victory. The very duration of the struggle, its appalling cost, should have opened most eyes to the falsity of the methods employed. Victory had come despite these methods, yet there was no change of heart. Once again military doctrines were conceived in flagrant contradiction with realities. Briefly, in the course of those twenty years France chose the defensive when she was strong and the offensive when she was weak. The climax came when, pledged politically to support various allies and neutrals in Europe, militarily her sole plan was to duck behind the Maginot Line, there to wait and see.

Immediately after the peace of 1919 France was left the most powerful nation in Europe. She chose the path of peace. It redounds to her honour; but that peace was based on mutual aid against aggression, and mutual aid implied the creation of an army ready to operate beyond her boundaries. Whereupon, paradoxically, she set about to reduce the term of compulsory service and to build the Maginot Line. Meanwhile Germany had clearly indicated her determination to free herself from the shackles of Versailles, to restore her armed might and, under Adolf Hitler, to gain hegemony over the entire continent, if not the world.

Nevertheless French military policy, determined by political and diplomatic policy, did not vary – pacific and defensive. Time after time it became manifest that mutual security, collective security, the League of Nations itself, were all postulated on the possibility of being able, at some time and in some place, to take forcible action in order to defend certain principles and impose them if need be. The invariable answer was "We have the Maginot Line behind which the nation can prepare for war". So it came to pass that whereas in 1914 "offensive à outrance" nearly spelled disaster, in 1940 "défensive à outrance" brought about the worst defeat in French history.

Again this resulted from the interplay of political, financial and military factors. The turning point should have come in 1936, when the Third Reich sent its troops into the Rhineland, demilitarised by treaty. The only possible answer on the French side was general mobilisation, which implied readiness to declare war. Both Government and High Command recoiled from the idea. No one wanted war. So nothing was done, beyond words. It is probable that mobilisation in 1936 would have checked Germany for a time, but it is doubtful whether it would have done more than delay the conflict which inevitably had to come. What the leaders of France's destinies failed to realise in 1936 was that military policy should be changed and that a purely defensive army no longer met the new situation.

Even some ten years before far-sighted observers had urged that a purely defensive concept was both absurd and dangerous – absurd because war is ever a combination of defence and offense; dangerous because it is too apt to impose on an army the sole notion of passive resistance and renders it incapable of that notion of offense without which victory cannot come. The purpose of war has remained the same through the ages – annihilation of the enemy.

So in September 1939 there assembled behind the Maginot Line a defensive army, in other words an army consisting of Reservists, in the proportion of almost four-fifths. In most infantry regiments three-fourths of the commissioned officers come from the Reserve. It follows that the bulk was not fully trained. Nor had it the necessary modern material. The same factors operated once again. A defensive army costs less, the argument ran; moreover there was the Maginot Line. It had meant much money and the outlay had not ended. Surely a policy of defence did not call for more than that. Let the Germans ruin themselves in constructing engines of war destined to be destroyed when they come to be used against the permanent fortifications lining the border. They would rue the day.

Certainly the Maginot Line was impressive. Early in the war many of its secrets were revealed in order to impress the French public with its strength. Newspaper correspondents were permitted to visit some of the works, resembling massive ironclads sunk into the earth, ready to belch forth fire at any invader. Certainly, those charged with its construction, General Charles Belhague and his engineers, had done their work well. Everything was complete – ventilation, protection against poison gas, communications, provisions, munitions, water supply, power plants; every detail was perfection itself. The motto on the badge of the garrisoning troops seemed justified: "No passage here".

There were tank traps and anti-tank cannon, machine-guns light and heavy, "75's" and heavier calibres, with ranges all registered in advance, all calculated to a nicety to ensure interlocking fire. In the intervals between works there were field fortifications manned by field troops. From Moselle to Rhine, all was ready to repel an assailant. The only flaw was that the assailant never came.

From the Moselle to the North Sea, to the West of the Maginot Line, more field fortifications had been built during the period from September 1939 to May 1940, with pill boxes and obstacles for tanks and many more devices. Behind this line were concentrated more forces, ready to meet the enemy should he decide to pass through Belgium. But on May 10, honourably answering Belgium's call, all these troops left their cover to march far into the Low Countries. They were beaten and the Maginot Line fell like a ripe plum, at once outflanked and attacked from the rear. Conceived to defend France, the Maginot Line in reality contributed in great measure to her undoing.

Both before 1914 and before 1939 there were men who had striven to combat the military doctrines in vogue. Prominent among them was Victor Constant Michel, commanding a brigade when I was in Nancy. Under fifty – quite young for a general officer in those days – he made a dashing, soldierly figure. His qualities were such that early in 1911 he was chosen as Commander-in-Chief. His tenure did not last more than six months – a tragedy with calamitous effects on the destinies of France. He was driven out on the pretext that he had lost his reason.

Official documents are either very reticent or very contradictory concerning this period; some even are not yet accessible to the student of military history. Yet by collating memoirs left by some of the principal actors, articles in newspapers and magazines, parliamentary reports and similar material, it is possible to approximate the truth. It seems clear today that if General Michel had not been called mad in July 1911 several major world problems might not have arisen. Possibly there might not have been a League of Nation and the relations of the United States with Europe might have been different, since it might not have taken part in the World War. Possibly, too, there might not have been a Soviet Russia. And very likely there would not have been a Battle of the Marne, won by General Joseph Jacques Césaire Joffre. For had Michel been heeded in 1911 it seems virtually certain that Joffre would have remained in that obscurity connoted by the fact that he had been designated a director of the Service of Supplies in case of hostilities. It is even conceivable that there might not have been a World War, at least not in 1914. And the Second World War was a direct consequence of the First.

His superiors as well as his peers called Michel mad because he forecast four things:

1) That in the event of war the Germans assuredly would attack France through Belgium

2) That once on Belgian territory they would not limit their operations to the right bank of the Meuse, but would cross the river in order to outflank the French

3) That the Germans would take the field with both Regulars and Reserve in the front line

4) That the German columns would be accompanied by heavy field artillery

As vice-president of the Higher War Council, which position carried with it supreme command in case of war, Michel's duty was to prepare the French campaign plan. He drafted Plan XVI, based solely on the defensive in the opening phases. Under this plan the French forces were concentrated behind both the Belgian and German frontiers; in addition Michel urged full utilisation of the Reserve and the provision of heavy field guns.

This was stirring the hornets' nest with a vengeance. Not that Michel was alone in foreseeing invasion through Belgium. Indeed, German intentions were plain to those who cared to read a map. Methodically the General Staff in Berlin had asked for the construction of highways and railroads all pointing to that end, roads which had no commercial value but which all radiated toward the borders of Belgium and

Luxemburg. Moreover at the very time when the French were dismantling fortifications, the Germans were striving to make Metz and Strasburg impregnable, to serve as pivot on their left for a vast encircling movement on their right. It was all so plain that in 1906 General Georges Lebon, then commanding the 1st Army Corps with headquarters at Lille, was moved publicly to demonstrate an evident truth and thereby to shatter all hope of promotion. The General Staff had prepared a war game in which he led the left wing with instructions to face east and cross the Moselle in order to simulate an offensive on German soil. Deliberately, Lebon deployed his troops along the Belgian border and waited. When taken to task he replied: "My information is that the enemy is attacking through Belgium". The war game ended abruptly.

Michel's Plan XVI was presented to the Minister of War in his capacity as president of the Higher Council and to the members of that body, all generals assigned to army commands if war occurred. They rejected it unanimously. Whereupon it was hinted that Michel was not in possession of all his faculties. He was compelled to resign. Joffre succeeded him. Three years later came terrible proof that there was much method in Michel's madness. Within two weeks of the declaration of war each of his four points were proved correct. In reality his most heinous offence had been the delivery of a public snub to the new school of thought. Ostentatiously he had announced that he would give a lecture at "the Field-Marshal's School". It turned out to be a systematic refutation of Grandmaison's teaching. When he ended there was dead silence amid which he left the hall with none to do him honour. From that day he was a marked man.

Joffre had been chosen as Michel's successor chiefly because he was considered "a democratic general". Two other candidates had been shelved, one (Pau) because he insisted on the prerogative of personally selecting his principal aides, the other (Castelnau) because he was "reactionary" in politics. Joffre was acceptable because he seemed modest, said little and was unassuming in manner and in dress even to the point of shabbiness. He had the reputation of being of the Left; moreover he was a Freemason, which in France then connoted radicalism and above all, anti-clericalism. At first he seemed subservient enough. For Plan XVI he substituted Plan XVII under which in August 1914, five armies rushed headlong to the frontier, engaged the enemy wherever found and were worsted all along the line. Joffre won undying fame by retrieving the situation with his victory on the Marne, but there is a blot on that fame – he retrieved a situation of his own making. For the Battle of the Marne he certainly deserved the laurel wreath, but it is a moot point whether he should not have been shot before, for losing the Battle of the Frontiers.

As it turned out, Joffre after the Marne was not so subservient as he had seemed. Victory had given him prestige which he exploited to the full. No one could have been more jealous of his authority; he was accused of repudiating the politicians who had set his foot in the stirrup; he seized every occasion to increase his power; he cashiered generals wholesale, in many cases for inefficiency, it is true, but also some who had been incautious enough to point out his errors. Nor did he disdain publicity; ambitious young officers who had hitched their wagon to his star saw to it that he had plenty. But gradually a cabal formed and in 1916, after several secret sessions of Parliament, he was kicked upstairs, made a Marshal of France and given a sinecure. Abandoning Freemasonry he died in the Catholic faith; the funeral service was at Notre-Dame Cathedral.

Joffre was replaced as commander-in-chief – with reduced powers – by General Robert Georges Nivelle, who had distinguished himself at Verdun by retaking the Forts of Vaux and Douaumont. And Nivelle's evil genius was Lieutenant-

Colonel Audemard d'Alençon, whom I had had as platoon commander at Nancy. Here again we have a tragedy.

Possibly the tallest man in the French Army, slim and sallow, d'Alençon was a strange man, even as lieutenant. He had passed through Staff College brilliantly and already he seemed more than conscious of his worth. To us in the ranks he appeared distant though courteous, but taciturn and moody, with few likeable traits, yet thoroughly efficient. By 1916, when I next had occasion to meet him, he had become even lankier and scraggier, a regular Knight of the Sorry Countenance.

D'Alençon had been assigned as Nivelle's assistant chief of staff. Soon he became his "chef de cabinet", a nondescript position, on the fringe of the regular establishment, but one of great power and authority. Few dare gainsay him when he said: "The Commander-in-Chief desires this or that to be done". Joffre had been reproached for his policy of attrition after the Marne and it had been agreed as a consequence that early in 1917 there should be a general offensive by the several Allies, each on his respective front. Nivelle felt that something more was expected of him and of the "young school of Verdun" which he represented. He came to believe that his tactics at Vaux and Douaumont – in reality localised raids on a large scale – could be applied on a wider front not only with success but with the certainty of breaking through and of exploiting that success to the full; he held out visions of a return to war of movement and of an early end to the campaign, with decisive victory.

His plan was to attack in force between Soisssons and Rheims, use heavy artillery – he himself was a gunner – to pound the whole depth of the enemy lines, and hold in reserve a mass of manoeuvre to operate in open country after all the trenches had been passed. Simultaneously the British would launch on their own front the offensive already agreed upon with Joffre in order to reduce German reinforcements. At G.H.Q. all the talk was of "rupture"; indeed the force that was to attack was called the Group of Armies of Rupture. At first this alluring plan was accepted with enthusiasm by many, though more reluctantly by some soberer minds. Enthusiasm dwindled as execution was delayed or hindered time after time – because of unfavourable weather, of hesitation among the executants, of voluntary withdrawal of the enemy to the Hindenburg Line. Yet Nivelle – with d'Alençon ever applauding – continued to have faith in his star. Doubters were treated with contumely. Difficulties rose with the British Commander-in-Chief, Sir Douglas Haig, who had been subordinated to Nivelle for the purpose of this offensive; rumour had it that the rift was caused by an imperious letter drafted by d'Alençon.

There were more delays, more hesitations; the Government became anxious and called a number of councils of war. But Nivelle and d'Alençon stood fast. By this time the "chef de cabinet", always inclined to be a visionary, had become a fanatical gambler on his chance. By this time also all France, both front and rear, was openly discussing a move, which depended on secrecy for success. Statements by German prisoners revealed cognisance not merely of the original plan but of many details. Still d'Alençon at G.H.Q. painted rosy pictures of a triumphant end to the war in the very near future. Again bad weather delayed execution. Again there was concern in high quarters. Nothing mattered. Nivelle had his way on April 16, 1917, in a snow-storm. The plan failed lamentably. The killed numbered 33 000 – over one hundred a minute between breakfast and lunch. Disillusion was complete; morale was severely tested, so severely indeed that there is a direct link between that April offensive and the mutinies of the following months. Nivelle was replaced by Pétain; d'Alençon went on sick leave and died in September. His son Marcel, lieutenant in the Air Force, was killed in aerial combat on the Somme in June 1940.

The third figure, Edouard de Curières de Castelnau, played a less tragic though no less important part in that war. In Nancy, I knew him as colonel commanding one of our infantry regiments. Short of stature, rather rotund, kindly and jovial, father of a large family, he was the very type of the Gascon soldier. It was difficult exactly to discuss why, but his unit was different. For instance, in the others the annual regimental fete was essentially military, austerely so. The men marched out to the rifle range to compete for shooting prizes; the only concession to frivolity was the issue of a ration of wine. Castelnau's regiment decorated barracks with garlands and greenery; there were shows, concerts, cake and ale, and, one memorable year, even some remarkable evolutions on stilts by men in fancy dress to lifting airs from "La Fille de Madame Angot". And men from other outfits were invited, to be made welcome by dapper sergeant-ushers in white gloves! Old martinets swore that the Service was going to the dogs!

Castelnau is still alive. His principal claim to fame is that he was one of the first to understand that the new doctrine had failed and he was wise enough and penitent enough to repudiate it. At Morhange he had seen my old Iron Division set out gallantly on bayonet charges, which ended in the mowing down of thousands by hidden machine-guns. He realised that though it might be magnificent it was not war, and of his own volition, under his own responsibility, he had ordered his troops to fall back pending the elaboration of other plans.

Castelnau, always deeply religious, never made a secret of his churchgoing; in later years he was known as "The Booted Friar". His career was distinguished – chief of staff, army commander, head of a group of armies – but his religious belief barred him from supreme command. A not inconsiderable body of public opinion thought he should have been made field-marshal for the Victory Parade in 1919. Possibly that might have been his reward had not the Armistice of November 11, 1918, intervened. For he had been given command of a group of armies which was to attack in Lorraine on November 14; the American Expeditionary Force was included in this group. I had a very modest part in the preparation and for days I saw long lines of trucks taking towards the front husky doughboys driven by diminutive Annamites. The object of the offensive was to rout the Germans and compel them to capitulate in the open field. Aware of their own demoralisation, they forestalled disaster by asking for cessation of hostilities. There followed the Treaty of Versailles, preluding the war of 1939. Had the Battle of Lorraine been fought, the whole course of History might have been changed. Here again is a lesson for today.

CHAPTER 5

NOBEL IS WHAT NOBEL DOES

Soldiering had certainly not advanced me in my chosen profession. Nor had it furthered my discovery of America or even my study of Democracy. It had been difficult to keep up with events. I had not spoken English for three years and it took some time for fluency to return. Apart from service reports I had written nothing and it was imperative to get into harness again. The only aid from military quarters was a certificate of honourable discharge, accompanied by a "fascicule de mobilisation" as constant reminder that war was possible, an ominous red card telling what to do and where to go when it was declared. In those days the rules were observed and there actually were declarations of war.

First I went back to Bedford. Everybody at the *Bedfordshire Times* was very nice; I received excellent testimonials - but no job. The truth is that from the English point of view I was handicapped by a deficiency. I did not write shorthand. I was conceded to be a competent copy-reader, an able writer. But managing editors in those days wanted more – they needed "shorthand reporters". Later, under American influence, progressive newspapers in England parted with tradition, but some conservative sheets long persisted in serving their readers that wearisome form known as oblique narrative. The "shorthand reporter" takes copious notes in the first person but transcribes them in the third: "Mr Jones said that they that night wished to welcome among them their active supporter Mr Smith". My better sense had always rebelled against the system and, possibly, for that reason, I could not for the life of me learn shorthand.

The inability irked me even more than the shorthand did. It created a feeling of inferiority, seeing that in all other branches I could hold my own. I think I understand why now. From my earliest days the speaker was my interest, not his words. And so indeed it is with most of us; the orator after all is akin to the actor or the singer. Too often he merely plays a part, poses, gesticulates, struts the stage even. Most orations when printed bore the reader; they lack the ephemeral life born of delivery. Yet the orator may take infinite pains, even rehearse before the mirror. I know of one man in particular – René Viviani. Today his name is forgotten. But on the strength of his speeches he rose to be Prime Minister. He was in office that fateful summer of 1914 when actions counted more than words. He lasted until October of the next year. In the spring of 1917 he accompanied Marshal Joffre on his mission to the United States.

In Paris Viviani used to prepare his speeches in the open air, in the streets adjoining the Parc Monceau, in which area he lived. People leaving the park at dusk might happen to see a stocky man muttering and posturing – the orator in the throes of creation. Occasionally he would stop to deliver himself of a mighty oath, for though polished in oratory he could be coarse in ejaculations. So it was in America. Emile Hovelaque, long Inspector-General of Education in modern Languages, who accompanied the mission as technical adviser, once told me this story.

By the time Joffre reached Chicago, Viviani had talked himself out. One evening he sent for Hovelaque, who found him nervously pacing his hotel room. "Hovelaque, old man, what in hell shall I tell them tomorrow? I can't go on like this, everlastingly repeating myself." Hovelaque, much cultured, of fastidious tastes, versed in Chinese lore, replied in the mood of "Confucius says": "Firstly these people are coming primarily to see Joffre, the Victor of the Marne, in flesh and blood. Secondly few understand French. Your part is that of the operatic tenor singing in his own language in a foreign land. It's your music they want, not your words."

That puts the case perfectly. Words, words, words! The world has been submerged by them. France especially. Some blame Julius Caesar for this. After his conquest of Gaul, they say, he encouraged a vogue for Cicero. Schools of eloquence were crowded. It was rhetoric in the final analysis that completed the subjection of the Gauls. Be that as it may after two thousand years Joffre the Taciturn has entered history, Viviani the Orator is forgotten.

To return to shorthand, it seemed such a waste of time to learn it when in the majority of cases only a summary of a speech was required. To me it seemed easier and better work to take occasional notes and then make a précis, rather than fill several pages with cabalistic signs and then laboriously transcribe a few extracts. Moreover shorthand tends to make you the slave of your notes.

I was compelled therefore to seek further afield. In December 1901 I received a letter signed: "Ralph Lane, Editor *Daily Messenger*, Paris", offering me a job as "assistant sub-editor" at a salary of 200 francs (40 gold dollars) monthly on condition that I joined at once. The letter specified that "shorthand was advisable but not absolutely essential". That relieved my mind. The pay was scarcely alluring, but within forty-eight hours I was in Paris.

Glamour – rather faded it is true – surrounded the *Messenger*. It was the successor of the famed *Galignani's Messenger* thanks to which Byron "awoke to find himself famous". It had been founded in 1814 by Giovanni Antonio Galignani, an Italian whose ancestors for three centuries had been either booksellers or bibliophiles or both. He had come to France towards the end of the Revolution but, for reasons of personal safety, had found it advisable to migrate to England, where his two sons were born. He returned later and in 1800 founded a bookstore, the forerunner of the well-known house on the rue de Rivoli. On July 2, 1814, he published the first issue of *Galignani's Messenger*, or *The Spirit of the English Journals* for the special benefit of the officers of Wellington's army of occupation. It was an immediate success and soon radiated to all those parts of Europe included by Englishmen in the traditional "grand tour". Eight months later Napoleon fled from Elba and during the Hundred Days the paper was suppressed. It had dared speak of "the Corsican Ogre!" But it reappeared after Waterloo, to last until 1904.

As its sub-title implied, *Galignani's* reprinted much from the English press. Giovanni Antonio had arranged for rapid delivery of papers brought by the Channel packets, several hours before they were available to individual subscribers, so that his news was always fresh. In addition it gave French items and information from other capitals. Soon it became known as the organ of Englishmen abroad. It had undoubted literary qualities. Several famous men of letters were on its staff at different times, including William Makepeace Thackeray, who "worked for ten francs a day and was very happy". So happy that he celebrated bouillabaisse in verse.

Although still enjoying considerable advertising patronage, especially from hotels in all parts of Europe, the *Messenger* was hit by constant progress in the transmission of news. It had been sold in 1890 by the heirs of the founder, and one of the conditions of sale was that the name of Galignani should be dropped. The *Daily Messenger* waned steadily until it died on July 29, 1904, in my arms so to speak, at the ripe age of ninety years.

When I called upon "Ralph Lane, Editor", I discovered the *Messenger* office and composing room – the paper was still hand-set – at the end of a gloomy court in the Faubourg Montmartre – a printing plant which contracted to bring out a number of papers and provided each with space in its building. This practice still obtains today. Ushered into a cubicle I found myself in the presence of a small man busily stitching at a length of canvas; Lane's recreation was sailing boats and he was mending a sheet.

Like Colonel d'Alençon, although only half his stature, Ralph Lane could have sat for a portrait of Don Quixote. Thin, blondish, with a scraggy beard, obviously in indifferent health and suffering from chronic sniffles, he seemed always absorbed in melancholy thought. His only concession to joviality was an occasional wry smile. He too was a visionary, by choice an "anti", tilting at the windmills of traditional conservatism. He was then feeling his way. It led him to a Nobel Peace Prize as Norman Angell (Angell was one of his father's given names) after he had written *The Great Illusion*, a best-seller in 1910. Returning to England, he became a Member of Parliament in the Labour interest and was knighted during one of J. Ramsay Macdonald's terms of office as Prime Minister. His Nobel Prize came in 1933 but he did not go to Oslo for his $44,338; report had it that he was "too busy".

When I knew him, the future Sir Norman was already busy compiling his first book, *Patriotism under Three Flags*, published in London in 1903. "Compilation" is the proper term since it comprised lavish quotations from speeches, newspaper editorials and review articles. Reading the volume again after nearly forty years, it scarcely indicates that the author was destined to become "a specialist in international affairs", as claimed in the English *Who's Who*. In the main it is an attack on Britain in connection with the Boer War, on the United States in connection with the Venezuelan boundary controversy and the Philippines, and on France in connection with the Dreyfus Affair. Here is a typical passage:

"It is not a mere effort of rhetoric but an absolute truth to say that there is not an act of tyranny, not a crime, not a cruelty which was alleged against Spain in her waging of the Cuban War as the justification of American intervention which America herself has not been guilty of in the Philippines ..."

He girds also at "the American desire to 'lick creation', to become 'a world power'", and he calls Admiral Alfred Thayer Mahan a "barbaric sentimentalist". There is also a curious reference to the London *Daily Telegraph* (then Jewish-owned) and its "racially alien proprietors". Beyond a doubt Angell would style himself a democrat, yet some of his writings tend towards totalitarianism. "Professional pacifist" would be a better description. There are plums in this as in most other professions.

Lane never was what is called a good mixer. He did not go among people, but sat in his office clipping newspapers and reviews, on which clippings – and not on life – he based all his theories. He had a craving for solitude; in later years he would go into retreat on a desert island off the coast of Essex of which he was practically the sole inhabitant. The weak point generally in Angell's arguments – at least it seems so to me – is that most of his theses are built on assumptions of which one may doubt. He is prone to consider States and Governments as individuals and to overlook the fact that, in democracies at least, their power and their policies spring from majority votes within. In 1914, not many weeks before the war, we lunched together in Paris and naturally discussed *The Great Illusion*. I recall that we could not agree, precisely because he left out the electorate in all his political dicta.

Lane in his way was something of a mystery. He was British-born but had lived many years in the United States; from casual conversation one concluded that he had become naturalised or at least received his first papers. His books sustained this view. Writing of his ranching days in California he invariably says "we" meaning Americans, and once he goes so far as to say: "I try to be a truly patriotic American". One judged that his ranching experiences had been a disappointment and that neither neighbours nor associates had proved congenial company. Be that as it may, he was accepted later as thoroughly English.

Work on the *Messenger* was pleasant enough – and there was plenty of it. Indeed there were quite long periods when Lane and I constituted the entire staff and he was generally much occupied with his book. That provided plenty of experience for a young man. In its way it was as valuable as it was strange. "Acrobatic" would be a fit term. For financial reasons our news sources were confined to the French papers and a three-minute telephone call with London, where a part-time man read out the headlines of the *Morning Leader*, now defunct. The very latest news came around 3 am, in the form of a brush-proof of the front page of a certain morning paper. How it reached us it was not my business to inquire. The report ran that for a stated sum each week one of the typographers would purloin the proof, fold it and put it in his pocket. Then he would go into the court to clean his hands – washroom facilities were rudimental in those days. There he tied the proof in a pig's bladder, threw it in the wash-tub, turned the faucet full and the resulting stream of water floated the bladder into the street, where a boy was ready to receive it. It is too good a story to lose, even if apocryphal.

We tried to crowd so much into those three minutes with London that occasionally things went awry. For instance we had a code for horse-race results. Our man at the other end would sing out a lot of figures which, if correctly received and interpreted after reference to the list of starters in *Sporting Life*, which reached us by the evening train form London, enabled us to print "full results from the tracks". One night, in my haste, I jumbled the dates, and the *Messenger* printed full results of the races to be run next day! Sir J. Blundell Maple, the furniture and racing magnate, and father-in-law of a German diplomat, happened to be in Paris at the time. Several of his horses were entered the next day and I had made them win by anticipation. He telephoned to point out the error and good-naturedly accepted our "results" as an omen. As it turned out, all his entries were beaten!

Lane's great newspaper hero was Edwin Lawrence Godkin, wherefore we subscribed to the New York *Evening Post* and clipped therefrom extensively to provide several "New York Letters" each week. Doubtless Godkin appealed to Lane because he also was an "anti", attacking everything, labour unions as well as trusts, Socialists as well as plutocrats. He appealed to me by his defence of free inquiry and free endeavour. The *Post* in my case was an introduction to mugwumps and other unsuspected aspects of American Life; it served also as an incentive to further exploration.

But the real value of the *Messenger* was that many interesting people found their way into its office to pass the time of day and exchange impressions. Journalism in Paris then was leisurely and inclined to be Bohemian. Americans, however, were far outnumbered by Britons. For Anglomania was still the vogue – English tailors, silversmiths and bars did good business. It was the heyday of English or pseudo-English store signs – Old England, The Hole in the Wall, His Lordship's Larder. And in the view of the average Frenchman an American was still deemed as essentially of British stock. In the 1900's Americans, in the mass, were beginning to discover France. It needed the First World War to speed the process.

For instance, when the Anglo-American Press Association of Paris was founded in 1907, there were then represented in the French capital eighteen British newspapers and four news agencies, compared with nine American papers and three news services. And at that some of the correspondents were free-lances serving several sheets. Moreover several still sent most of their matter by mail rather than by the expensive cable. From the journalistic point of view it was a period of transition, in which very definite American influences were to be discerned.

On the British side there was a phalanx of noted correspondents of the old school, led by Stephan de Blowitz, of the London *Times*, bewhiskered, gnome-like and fast going blind, and Thomas T. Farman, of the *Standard*, now extinct, whose sons, Richard, Henry and Maurice, became prominent in the development of the automobile and the airplane in France. There was also Mrs Emily Crawford, who had taken her late husband's succession as correspondent of the *Daily News*, the first woman to serve abroad for any London paper. That they knew how to get news had been proved by Blowitz' legendary exploits – in 1878 he had obtained the text of the Treaty of Berlin and printed it before the Foreign Office knew that it had even been signed – but their despatches were in the nature of articles, more or less editorial, rather than news reports. And they looked askance at the telephone, preferring the telegraph or even the mails. At the *Messenger* we saw more of the younger school of correspondents, the go-getters of the fast-rising *Daily Mail* and *Daily Express*; in professional outlook they were much closer to their American colleagues than to their compatriots. And they telephoned with gusto!

The conception of foreign news was evolving on the American side also. So far as newspapers were concerned, the packet-boat era was closing. Correspondents in Europe had been accustomed for the most part to write elaborate letters reflecting political and diplomatic trends, rather than plain reports of events. They would send these letters by boat, together with occasional interviews with leaders in various fields. Nevertheless, interviewing, then at its peak, was rather the province of special correspondents – Richard Harding Davis and Price Collier among them – who came armed with letters of introduction from the State Department and passed several weeks calling on European celebrities.

Mostly under the influence of the *New York Herald*, the entire staff of whose European Edition acted as a sort of omnibus correspondent, more and more importance became attached in New York to foreign intelligence, and a new school of correspondents developed. Such men as Stoddard Dewey, Theodore Stanton and Lamar Middleton witnessed the transition and readily adapted themselves to changing conditions. Moreover, representatives of the younger generation were appearing in Paris. At least one remained an expatriate – A. Warrington Dawson, then attached to the Scripps-McRae League, precursor of the United Press. After accompanying Theodore Roosevelt on his African hunts, he became a chronic invalid and blossomed into a leading citizen of Versailles. There was also Arthur Lynch, in a category to himself. This ardent Irish soul had espoused the Boer cause in the war with England and had come back as "Colonel" Lynch. Tried and condemned for treason, he had been pardoned, then married Maud Gonne, who led the agitation in Paris in favour of Free Ireland. He settled down for a time, writing for English and American newspapers, but politics claimed him and he left France, subsequently to represent an Irish constituency in Parliament in London.

From conversations with these and others, the young explorer of American thought and American ways learned much. They introduced him, moreover, to an inexhaustible source of information and interest – the magazines of the United States, monthlies and weeklies. The main attraction resided in the advertisement pages. Long experience has taught me this: You cannot know a city until you have roamed through its markets; neither can you hope to know America if you ignore American advertisements. For many years now magazines from the United States have piled up on my desk; never has one been discarded without a glance at the advertising; the reading matter is of less consequence. Martin Sommers, of the *Saturday Evening Post*, certainly will bear me out.

In those days, too, the illustrations caught my attention. Photo-engraving had not yet invaded every field and American illustrators well held their own. Apart from technical qualities, their work in many cases struck a new note, essentially American. Indeed American art occupies a prominent place in my exploration; there will be other references to it. Nor were books neglected – mostly borrowed, for the *Messenger's* ten dollar a week did not go so far as in Thackeray's time. They included Motley, Prescott, Bryant, Holmes, Whitman, and above all that confirmed individualist Thoreau. During the First World War my campaign library was necessarily of the lightest but it included "Walden".

If for Norman Angell the *Messenger* was to lead to a Nobel Peace Prize, so far as I was concerned it determined the path I was to follow. It provided furthermore opportunities to meet another winner of the Prize. In all the political agitation of those days one man began to stand out – Aristide Briand, then an obscure deputy who in the course of time headed more Cabinets than any political leader before him, became an apostle of peace through collective security and a bulwark of the League of Nations. It has yet to be determined how far he

75

was a cynic, how far sincere. At all events, it is sufficiently clear today, despite the activities of the newspapers' thurifers and lavish outpourings "for propaganda" from the millions placed at the disposal of the Quai d'Orsay as "secret funds", that he fell victim to the "finessiering" of Gustav Stresemann – the "good old Stresemann" of Locarno days. Briand's great assets were dulcet tones in oratory ("Now I'll give them some of my violoncello notes", he would say when preparing to intervene in a menacing debate) and uncanny ability to rally waverers in the lobbies before a vote.

At that time Briand was a struggling journalist and attorney – and definitely an extremist. He wrote articles for an American sheet, edited an anticlerical daily, defended in the courts striking workers with violent revolutionary pleadings, so violent that they were veritable appeals to civil war. When the *Daily Messenger* had gone to press a favourite meeting place was a tavern at the corner of the Rue Montmartre and the Rue du Croissant, then the Newspaper Row of Paris. It never closed day or night; journalists and typographers could always eat a bite there, and the beer was good. On the way to the Croissant one often met Briand, shaggy of head and lip, shabby of dress, slouching of gait, ever smoking cigarettes – he rolled his own in those days.

Soon Briand made his mark by steering through the Chamber of Deputies the bill separating Church and State. He remained shaggy to the end and consumed ever more cigarettes. But he mended his slouch and grew sprucer as success came. Berthe Cerney, a pretty actress form the Comédie Française, had taught him étiquette and deportment. The man who had shouted in court that he was prepared to lead rebellious workers, waving the red flag, began to wear a tuxedo. The man who had to live down a past – an amorous adventure in a meadow when he was still struggling for recognition at Nantes – now hobnobbed with archbishops and dowagers round the tea table.

He became Minister, Prime minister, apostle of a peace plan – suggested to him by an American newspaper man – and even came to believe that so long as his dulcet voice spoke – "Get back you cannon! Get back you machine-guns!" – there could be no war. Simultaneously he had become less and less extreme, dropping the Socialist label and registering in the Chamber as an independent non-party man. Apotheosis came with his death – a State funeral and a monument on the Quai d'Orsay. But the monument was for the most part plaster, fast flaking off the last time I saw it as my party joined the Great Exodus. He had his Nobel Prize – and war came none the less.

In France in those days – and later – law and journalism were regular stepping-stones to a political career and many men whose names are now written in history foregathered in that corner café. Generally they sought new haunts as they rose in the world. There was one, however, who remained faithful to the Croissant – Jean Jaurès, Socialist tribune of the people. He had his favourite table, whereat he was seated when he was shot dead on the outbreak of war in 1914. A tablet on the house-front recalled the fact. Now the old-fashioned tavern has given way to a glittering modern bar.

Soon I ceased to frequent the Croissant myself, for the good reason that the *Messenger* came to a sudden end. It still enjoyed a measure of advertising patronage, especially from Continental hotels catering for tourists, and it still had a fair number of readers. But operating costs increased steadily while revenues declined. Less and less could be spent on news, though Heaven knows we were by no means prodigal in that department. Diligent collection of advance notices enabled us to make that three-minute telephone call with London go a very long way.

So adept had we become in this work that on one occasion our only competitor, the European Edition of the *New*

York Herald, took alarm and there were changes in its editorial staff. That was in May, 1903, when May Goelet married the Duke of Roxburghe, one of the first American girls to wear a coronet. Our man in London read out: "Roxburghe Marriage. Bride cuts Wedding Cake with Groom's Sword". That was sufficient cue. Out came the collection of clippings. And next morning the *Herald's* 300 words, honestly cabled, were shamed by a full column in the *Messenger*, "From our own Correspondent".

We did even more wonderful things with that three-minute conversation. We had close relations with the *Éclair* (yet another paper now dead) in whose building we were housed. Each night from that call we supplied its foreign editor with "Latest News from London", frequently reproduced by the *Temps* and other evening sheets – and on occasion telegraphed to London as authoritative comment "From the best-informed French circles".

This connection with the *Éclair* was of help in my discovery of America. Occasionally I was asked to interview American personalities passing through Paris. They ranged from Colonel William Hester, publisher of the *Brooklyn Daily Eagle*, to John Alexander ("Profit") Dowie. From the former I obtained an inkling of the intricacies of American politics – Theodore Roosevelt was then standing for another term – while from the latter I gained an insight into the possibility of launching in the United States any scheme, however freakish, so long as it was well publicised. These early lessons left me rather bewildered but eager for more.

But even such acrobatics could no more than prolong the agony. Ralph Lane announced one day that he had acquired control of the sheet; he seemed rather hurt when I seized the occasion to ask for more money. Hitherto the publisher, one Kayzer, had maintained Olympian detachment for the common mortals who laboured for him. But the change of regime did not change conditions. So, because no one would pay the printer, the *Daily Messenger* died on July 29, 1904. A very small but very loyal staff insisted on preparing the forms and seeing them placed on the press. But the press never turned.

Next morning, at the publishing office in the Rue Saint Honoré, elderly English subscribers, not a few maiden ladies among them, bewailed its passing: "We have nothing now but that horrid *New York Herald*". But a phoenix was to arise from the ashes. The first number of the *Continental Daily Mail* appeared on May 22, 1905. The last editor of the *Messenger* was Ralph Lane, and Ralph Lane was the first editor of the *Continental Daily Mail*. Soon he wrote *The Great Illusion*; it appealed to his boss, Alfred Harmsworth, who supported it with the very wide publicity at his command. A Nobel Prize loomed on the horizon.

In a sense the *Mail* was the *Messenger* in a new incarnation. Not only was there the same editor, but in its swaddling days the newcomer was printed in the very place where the *Messenger* had been printed. Moreover many men of the editorial, advertising and mechanical staffs were retained to work for the new venture, and the hotel advertising was retrieved. For my part I went to "that horrid *Herald*". Later I was invited to secede, but the die was cast. I became American.

CHAPTER 6

INTOLERANT LIBERTY

In the meantime I had begun another exploration – that of my own country, of French thought and trends. Random philosophic readings, the legend of the Great Revolution, a craving for all liberties after three years of Army life, had left my political creed still chaotic. I had dipped into P.J. Proudhon, Charles Fournier, Karl Marx even Kropotkin, and the way to a better world – even to the ideal world – yet seemed to be Blanqui's way, going into the street with muskets, setting up barricades and seizing power, whereupon a new era would dawn, an era of justice and brotherly love. All sympathies were instinctively with the Left, with Dreyfusists, Socialists, even Anarchists.

To a young mind, for instance, there could be no nobler figure than Jean Grave; a self-educated compositor, blond-bearded and everlastingly wearing a black overall, he indeed loved his fellow-man and gave all he had – little enough in all conscience – to needy comrades while he himself lived miserably, for the sake of the Cause. He was an Anarchist at a time when Anarchism was the vogue among bourgeois youth, but to the last he alone practiced it in the form of charity and tolerance.

Tolerance! At the outset investigation of my own country and of my own people had disconcerting aspects. It was only in later years that I discovered Oliver Cromwell's dictum on liberty: how every sect clamours for it, but once having it denies it to all others. Intolerance conjoined with envy helped to bring about the downfall of France. And at this writing at least intolerance and envy have merely changed camps, with Pierre Laval helping.

My investigation soon showed bureaucracy facing one at every turn, absurd, wooden, tyrannical. In theory officials should have been servants and helpers of the people; in reality they abused the modicum of authority devolving upon them so that they might browbeat and hinder. The Revolution and Napoleon had left France a singular heritage – centralisation, codification and classification, with all their attendant documents. A Frenchman accumulates "papers" from birth to death. His every act is regulated by ordinances and instructions. This is even truer of the New Order under Pétain than it was of the old. The walls throughout the land are placarded with them. They may be disregarded or forgotten, but they exist, wherefore they can always be produced, either to support or to refute. In bygone days, nothing more astonished Americans coming to France than this insistence on the production of "papers" for the simplest acts of daily life. But there was something more serious than this nuisance.

Liberty in my mind had been associated with tolerance. On the other side of the English Channel it had been permissible to listen in Hyde Park to soap-box orators denouncing Royalty – and that under the protection of the police. The idea seemed to be that the best way to dispose of such is to let them speak. Certainly, it would have been rash to draw general conclusions from this fact; nevertheless it was a symbol. In France we preferred other symbols, expressed in words, the more eloquent the better. At the opening of the 20th century I found France disappointingly intolerant.

The Dreyfus Affair was over, but it had left antisemitism in its wake. To this was added a revival of

81

anticlericalism. Never since the Revolution had such a violent campaign been waged against religion. In France anticlericalism has generally been purely a political manifestation. To comprehend, you must remember that the Revolution dates no further back than 150 years and that there have been crowded into the intervening period experiments with every possible form of government, every possible political or economic nostrum, accompanied by every possible calamity – dictatorships, empires, kingdoms (by divine right as well as by popular will), republics; inflation, devaluation, managed economy, forced labour, unemployment; new calendars, new weights and measures, new systems of administration, of justice and of religion; conservatism, liberalism, radicalism, socialism, communism, anarchism; plebiscites, insurrections, blood purges, civil strife; a Mexican adventure, a Dreyfus Affair, and several wars with invasion of the national territory. By the time France celebrated the 150th anniversary of the fall of the Bastille, she had been surfeited with events. She suffered from a chronic complaint – an ill-digested French Revolution.

National life had been marked by so many upheavals that the average man was never sure of his ground. Although he asserted that he had become a free man, there were moments when he feared that it might all be a dream and that he would awaken to find himself still a serf in revolt. To convince himself of his emancipation he addressed his fellows as "Citizens", he inscribed "Liberty, Equality, Fraternity" on his monuments, he discoursed on the Rights of Man and on the Federation of Mankind, he named his battleships "Democracy" or "Justice". Politically, he progressed from liberal to radical, from radical to socialist, from socialist to communist. It was a token of emancipation to go over to the Left, ever farther from the old shibboleths. Above all it was a token of emancipation to deny the existence of the Deity. "Ni Dieu ni maître" – no God nor master.

So atheism and anticlericalism developed into a political doctrine. In their rage for destroying all forms of tyranny, the Jacobins professed to liberate man from spiritual as well as from material thrall. For God Robespierre substituted "Reason". From this day the notion persisted that republicanism must be irreligious. The Radical Party (later Radical-Socialist), the party of Georges Clemenceau, of Edouard Herriot, of Edouard Daladier, which for years guided the destinies of the Third Republic, prided itself on its Jacobin descent; consequently it was anticlerical. By waging war on religion, it succeeded for a long time in concealing its opportunism, its lack of a constructive program. Eventually it brought about the separation of Church and State; that was in 1905, the period of my early survey.

That being so, it had come to pass that religion drew a great line of demarcation in France. There were of course middle parties comprising both godly and godless. They represented a force to be considered in every case but one – on religious issues there could be no middle course. Moreover "laïcité" became a touchstone even beyond politics. "Laïcité" is difficult to render into English. From its original meaning of "lay" it came to denote neutrality and then evolved into avowed godlessness. The godly stood on the Right; they called themselves liberal, but the godless dubbed them reactionaries. In general terms the Left knew not God, at least not in public.

Yet the homely comparison still held true; your average Frenchman resembled a Dutch cheese – deep red without but very white within. So when calamity followed upon calamity after that fateful May 10, 1940, even the godless were awed. Just as on their deathbeds many anticlericals had feared to pass into the presence of their Maker without the ministration of a priest, so the "lay" leaders of a reputedly "lay" State stood with bowed heads in Notre-Dame Cathedral while the nation prayed to God to deliver France. And they spoke glibly of Christian morality in the conduct of affairs, whether individual or collective.

This Day of National Prayer marked a recantation. Since November 9, 1906, the French State had abjured God. On that day, in the Chamber of Deputies, René Viviani had spoken thus on behalf of the Cabinet:

"The French Revolution unleashed in man all the daring of his conscience and all the ambition of his thought. That was not enough. The Revolution of 1848 endowed man with universal suffrage; it raised the labourer bowed under his task and made of the humblest the political equal of the mightiest. That was not enough. The Third Republic summoned around it the sons of peasants and the sons of labourers, and into these obscure minds, into these endarkened consciences, it instilled gradually the revolutionary germ represented by education. That was not enough.

We all, by our fathers, by our elders, by ourselves, have been identified in the past with a work of irreligion. We have torn human consciences away from belief. When wearied by the burden of the daily task, when a poor weight bowed the knee, we raised him and told him that behind the clouds there were nothing but chimeras. Altogether, in a magnificent gesture, we have extinguished in the heavens beacons that will never be lighted again."

Fine words these! They drew cheers, prolonged again and again. And the Chamber in its enthusiasm voted that the speech should be printed and posted on the walls of every community in the land. On the strength of his extinguishing, Viviani became famous and in the natural order of things rose to Premiership. Wits recalled how another unbeliever, Henri Rochefort, the brilliant pamphleteer who had done much to sap the Second Empire, had himself satirized such manifestations. He had parodied a decree thus:

"Article First – God is hereby suppressed.

Article Second – The Minister of Public Worship is entrusted with the application of this decree."

The beacon of faith having been extinguished, it was normal that the test of "laïcité" should be extended to every phase of French life. Thus in literature there were "Writers of the Right" and "Writers of the Left". Even painters were so classified. Scientists also; at the death of Edouard Branly, the physicist, Left papers studiously refrained from mentioning that for years he had been a professor at the Catholic Institute. And in the Army there were "Republican generals" and "Reactionary generals". Because he went to church, Ferdinand Foch, destined to lead the Allies to victory in 1918, saw his promotion retarded by "lay" governments in the years before the First World War. The Second World War brought a truce, at least so far as the Radicals were concerned, but the Socialists in their turn began to raise the anticlerical cry.

This trend had far-reaching consequences; for one thing it influenced the drafting of the Treaty of Versailles in 1919. For although it had been averred many years before by a great Radical leader, Léon Gambetta, that "anticlericalism is not an article for exportation", inevitably it tinged foreign policy as well as domestic. At Versailles, the creation of a Czechoslovak State was welcomed by Left elements since, in their view, it would represent "a focus of 'laïcité' in Central Europe". Similarly these elements advocated partition of the Austro-Hungarian Empire because it was Catholic in the main. For, although ostensibly directed against all denominations, French anticlericalism was always essentially anti-Catholic. It may be added that men of the Left in France never quite understood

85

how British leaders so close to them in political thought, such as J. Ramsay Macdonald and George Lansbury, could reconcile Socialistic principles with church-going. And it may be suspected that Woodrow Wilson's Christian faith was not foreign to Clemenceau's allusion to his "noble candour".

All this serves to throw light on that intolerance I so sorrowfully discovered in the 1900's. Emile Combes had become Prime Minister and was applying a strictly anticlerical program which was nothing less than repudiation of certain liberties – liberty of education, of association, of thought. The climax came with the revelation of the existence of a card index classifying Army officers according to their political opinions and religious practices. Things improved in the next forty years but a certain measure of intolerance persisted until September 1939. It still pained one to hear political leaders, even those in the highest places, place party before country and, when they spoke of "Republican order" and "Republican liberties", implied exclusion from the fold of those who did not hold their views. Democracy surely cannot be synonymous with conformism.

Nor should democracy be synonymous with hatred or envy. Liberty is difficult enough to assure. What of equality? Certainly there cannot be equality of birth. America prides herself on offering equality of opportunity, most laudable if it implies levelling up. In France, unfortunately, the trend was to level down. In a fine gesture on August 4, 1789, the Constituent Assembly renounced all individual privileges in order to abolish class distinctions. Henceforth, it was proclaimed, men were indeed to be equal. Then for the next 150 years men strove to regain privileges for themselves while denying them to others. The consequence was to create more and more political parties, each of which had but a single aim – to attain office in order to share the spoils.

In this the Radicals excelled. Tammany Hall is virtually limited to New York. The Radical Party extended its operations over the length and breadth of the land. For forty years it was a power to be reckoned with, and for forty years its local committees were active – finding jobs, relieving distress, distributing favours, marshalling voters. No Radical ever applied in vain to his organisation. With a very long spoon it doled out the gravy. The power of the Radical Party increased from the fact that it furnished the rank and file of Freemasonry, which in France has ever been closely allied with politics and with anticlericalism.

An early act of the Pétain Government in 1940 was to suppress Masonry through a law directed against "secret societies". The Masons were intolerant; the anti-Masons even more so. With deft use of propaganda it was suggested that in every walk of life Freemasonry had been sapping the very foundations of the community – the same outcry which had been raised against the Jesuits one hundred years before. Masons were pilloried in the *Journal Officiel* as a prelude to being ousted from all public posts. They had been intolerant to others. Now they found no tolerance. But there was an anti-climax: in all seriousness it was revealed that there were only 100 000 Masons in a population of forty million. There were then other manifestations of intolerance, mostly imposed by the victorious Germans – the measures against Jews for instance.

Meanwhile, by 1939, there had developed some twenty parties or groups, sub-parties and sub-groups, each putting party before country (the Socialists made a point of printing party with a capital letter and country with a small one) and each fighting the other for power, openly or covertly. Periodically coalitions were formed; they seldom achieved anything because of the internecine struggles. All were suspicious one of the other, so that coalitions were ephemeral, soon to resolve themselves again into mutually aggressive component parts. All of which did not contribute to faith in the third element of the Republic's motto: "Fraternity".

Bluntly put, each party, each group, each sub-party, each sub-group was out for spoils. And the prime purpose of each was to limit the number of participants. Intolerance was not only religious but political. It culminated in Léon Blum's historic: "I hate you!" hurled in a debate in the Chamber of Deputies. When the consequent uproar abated, he hastened to add: "Or rather I hate your ideas". Whichever way you take it, "hate" was the key-word. All the more so since he had made it plain that if ever he came to power "legality would be given a holiday".

Of the many French Prime Ministers I have met, Blum was no worse – and no better – than any of the others, André Tardieu, Pierre Laval, Edouard Herriot, Edouard Daladier, Paul Reynaud, Pierre Etienne Flandin. All were party men – and all were intolerant. I first knew Blum in the old *Herald* days when we worked in cooperation with the *Matin*. At the offices of that paper one occasionally saw the drama critic, a tall, spare man, invariably well-groomed, wearing pince-nez, wide-brimmed hat, peg-top trousers and very small-sized shoes. A dainty handkerchief protruded from his breast pocket. In conversation attention went to his expressive hands, ever twining and untwining. He signed his articles "Guy Launay" but that was an omnibus by-line; at that time "Launay" was really Léon Blum.

He belonged to an esoteric circle of aesthetes of which the outward and visible sign was the Rembrandt-like hat, the scarf double-wound which served as cravat, and a general air of aloofness. Had France had an Oxford University, Blum and some others might have become counterparts of George Nathaniel Curzon, that "very superior person". Blum was not averse to scandalising the bourgeois mind. He frequented a literary salon of the Left, that of Mme Arman de Caillevet, where Anatole France held forth in phrases blending the classic with the erotic. He contributed to the *Revue Blanche* iconoclastic articles which paved the way for his brochure: "On Marriage", in which he counselled young girls to know as many men as possible before wedlock and hinted, as De Quincy had done of murder, that incest might be considered one of the fine arts. In addition, he reviewed books for the then Socialist *L'Humanité*.

Blum came of a family of Jewish silk factors but he had sought a career in the Civil Service; he held a position in the Council of State which assured him a pension, even while under detention for "betraying its trust". Ostensibly a Socialist, of the international variety – the French Socialist Party always stressed that it belonged to the Second International – he was ever an aristocrat in his tastes. He loved antique silver and good table appointments. One of his American biographers went into raptures at the revelation that he knew how to use a fish-knife.

When he turned to politics he was irked by the promiscuity of public meetings in the populous quarters of Paris. Later, as a water-drinker, he could not stoop to join his Narbonne electorate in quaffing the thick red wine of the region. He remained an aesthete – effeminate in some traits – though he was not above realisation of the immense administrative patronage which the French system of centralisation conferred on each member of the Government.

Léon Blum may have had many faults. All spring from the fact that he is a doctrinaire, and, what is more, a doctrinaire with the courage of his convictions – physical courage if need be. In addition he is a casuist, ever ready to split straws, a man of study but scarcely one of action. Party and doctrines have meant everything to him; indeed he was prepared to set them before country, even before duty. And his fecund imagination led him to believe that he could stoop to be one of the people though at heart he disdained plebeians. A true disciple of Jean-Jacques Rousseau, he wanted to compel the masses to be free.

Léon Blum thrives in opposition and fails in office, for his casuistry necessarily is destructive and his construction is entirely on an abstract plane. Never were his intelligence and his talent so manifest as in February 1942 when he appeared at Riom before the Supreme Court specially created by Marshal Pétain – ill-advised in this circumstance as in so many others – to try "the men responsible for the defeat of French arms" – five in all. The limitation was too utterly preposterous. Responsibility rested on a system, on a mentality, not on individuals.

Blum had been under detention many months, and rumour had it that his health had suffered. There was no sign of this when he appeared before his judges as well-groomed as ever, erect despite his years and quietly defiant. The only flaw was a woollen scarf of hideous hue – the weather was bitterly cold. But he removed it as soon as seated, whereafter he was his old self. His opening address was a feat of reason, his legal argumentations beyond praise. Yet, he could not surmount a weakness inherent in so many intellectuals, dangerous because it is a form of vanity – an irrepressible desire to know: "How far have I impressed?" And he would turn to right and left as if to seek applause. Edouard Daladier, of far inferior mental calibre, irked his judges much more by forgoing subtleties and doggedly facing them.

As head in 1936 of the first Popular Front government in France, Léon Blum had envisioned a democratic millennium under the leadership of an aristocrat, both on the material and intellectual planes. Very possibly he was sincere when he imagined he heard popular cries of joy making the welkin ring as he initiated certain social reforms, but he closed his eyes to the fact that the so-called democrats in his wake wore kid gloves, ate and drank of the best and disported themselves as the salt of the earth while the common folk continued to suffer as before. These common folk, with many desires but slender means, came to accuse the social structure of withholding their due share of things. Having lost all taste for labour, all confidence in individual effort, they looked upon the State as universal provider. And the State failed them. There were too many calls on the public purse. Thus are defeats prepared; they beget new forms of government not more tolerant than the old.

Anyway, while Léon Blum was still struggling for recognition, I was studying totalitarianism in the person of James Gordon Bennett the younger.

CHAPTER 7

<u>INTRODUCING MRS PEABODY</u>

The status of the *New York Herald* (European Edition) as a newspaper was such, and its owner James Gordon Bennett the younger had such a reputation for whims, that after the demise of the *Daily Messenger* I hesitated several months before seeking employment in that quarter. In the meantime I found occasional work helping British correspondents or replacing them when on vacation, incidentally making my debut in American journalism by writing a few "Paris Letters" for the *Pittsburgh Dispatch*, yet another addition to my list of defunct newspapers. My hesitation was understandable when you recall the characteristics of the Paris *Herald* and the innumerable eccentricities attributed to its master. That is the correct word, for Bennett ruled his "rich man's toy" with despotic hand. Both Bennett's *Heralds* have gone also, merged with the *Tribune*.

He had founded his European Edition on October 4, 1887. He had imagined that London would appreciate an English edition of his great New York organ, but London did not smile upon him. It was much too early for Americanisation of the English press, later so avid to Americanise itself. Paris took more kindly to American methods, but it must be confessed that in the course of the years Bennett and his *Herald* became less and less American and more and more French. The space devoted to "mondanités" (society items) became greater and greater. They were printed in French and the principal contributors were French – or Italians living in Europe. Reports of racing in France were printed in French, as were also the debates in the Chamber of Deputies, the weekly survey of the Paris Bourse and reviews of French books. At Easter and at Christmas the *Herald* issued ambitious supplements, printed partly in colour. The principal contributions were by French authors of mark such as Anatole France and Paul Bourget and were written in French; the principal illustrations were reproductions of works by leading French painters.

As a consequence the number of Continental subscribers surpassed at one time those of Anglo-Saxon origin. The reproach was levelled at Bennett's sheet that it was not an American paper. But he could afford to ignore such reproaches, for it was on the strength of its Continental clientele that the *Herald* obtained the major part of its advertising. The fact that nearly every crowned head in Europe – there were many then – subscribed to the paper was a strong argument to advance when soliciting advertisements from the luxury trades. It followed logically that the *Herald,* in its classified advertisements, had many under the head "domestic help": butlers, valets, footmen, maids. No French organ could equal it in this respect.

But personal news was not restricted to the French section of the paper. The inherent danger in the matter of printing names is that there is no limit. You begin by printing ten and very soon print a hundred; the hundred grow into a thousand. And still they come. Some issues of Bennett's *Herald* contained infinitely more names than any other matter – names of guests at luncheon or dinner parties, names of people arrived at hotels in Paris, in Berlin, in London, on the Riviera – names of people arriving in Timbuktu had there been hotels in Timbuktu in those days; names of passengers on liners; names of persons arriving from America and names of people going to America; names of people buying automobiles and names of people buying dogs; letters from Nice, Cannes and Monte Carlo filled with names; letters from every resort, fashionable or not fashionable, filled with names; names of people touring "en automobile", of people cruising on yachts. Names and names and names, copied for the greater part by hotel porters and shipping clerks and too frequently copied inaccurately. Some could be checked and corrected; the majority could not – they were printed as received.

The inner workings of the *Herald* were somewhat of a puzzle, if not of mystery. Few of its staff frequented journalistic haunts. At the *Daily Messenger* we were visited occasionally by John Parslow, who might have stepped out of a Dickens book – a lovable old tippler periodically fired and rehired, very English in his old-fashioned frock-coat and top hat, courteous, cultured, but an unmitigated nuisance in his cups. One met also Gordon Gordon Smith, a burly Scot who specialised in the politics of Central and Eastern Europe, as well as military subjects. This background prepared him for the most unexpected climax to a newspaper career – "Acting military attaché of the Yugoslav Legation in Washington".

But none of the *Herald* men had much to tell of Bennett, beyond repeating hoary anecdotes. This was no cause for surprise since few approached Bennett often enough really to know him. Following his death in 1918 the authors of several books claimed to have been his familiars; even today, especially in obituary notices, it is said of this or that old-timer that he was Bennett's trusted executive and confidant. The truth is that Bennett would have liked very much to dispense with executives. It was characteristic of his masterful ways that he would have no managing editor. Since he seldom went to America, he reluctantly conceded a measure of authority to a "city editor" in New York; in Paris he had an "editor-in-charge" liable at any moment to be reduced to the ranks. For advisers he had no room. Bennett was the *Herald* and the *Herald* was Bennett. He could be generous on occasion, but not to the extent of sharing his powers.

James Gordon Bennett the Younger might have done great things had he been compelled to blaze his own trail. His father had fought the fight of life and had learned much in the fighting. He was a force. Reviled, even horsewhipped, he went his way and completed the newspaper revolution he had initiated in a basement in Wall Street, writing his articles on the barrel which served as cash box. At his death the *New York Herald* stood at the forefront. The son never knew that life. Even as a boy he was not allowed to mix with other boys, punching heads and having his head punched. As he grew older – and inherited millions – his acquaintance with the world was limited to a number of friends and to the sycophants who pressed around him. Genuine admiration for his father led him to follow in much the same lines, but he had his own flashes of inspiration, as when he sent Stanley to Africa, relieved famine in Ireland and sent an expedition – ill-fated – to the Arctic. At times his instinct would tell him where news would break and he would have a reporter on the spot; at other times his hesitation, his suspicion of all about him would prevent his staff from giving their best.

Despite his European ways and his inconsistencies, Bennett was considered in Europe to typify American journalism; in reality he was an expatriate who had "gone native" and his paper was cosmopolitan. Thanks in part to the glamour surrounding its owner, the Paris *Herald* waxed strong. In the years immediately preceding the First World War, when my duties permitted access to figures, I discovered that it was making money in spite of lavish expenditure. Indeed there is reason to believe that it had actually shown a profit almost from the start. But its master preferred that people should think otherwise. Balance-sheets – there were none until he decided to form a nominal company on whose board of directors he gave me a seat – invariably showed a loss, it is true, but that was because of Bennett's social and other obligations in his own peculiar way. Some "society correspondents" figured on the editorial pay-roll for no other reason – and their remuneration was princely. In Venice, for instance, he had met the Countess Morosini, much admired by the then German Emperor (Wilhelm II); her lady companion became titular Venetian correspondent at a yearly salary of 2 400 dollars gold.

It seems furthermore that he believed he could ward off competition by showing steady losses – on paper. When he had wind of a probable invasion of the continental field by Alfred Harmsworth's *Daily Mail*, he imagined he could frighten him off on the score of cost. The *Herald* printed editorials descanting on the long purse required for such a venture and enumerating the sums spent on its news services. Using Chinese tactics – China, too, has changed since – Bennett brought out a horrific dragon in the hope of scaring his potential rival. Had Harmsworth needed spurring, this attitude would have served most effectively. He hit back in an editorial in the first issue of his *Continental Daily Mail*, announcing that it had "financial resources not exceeded by any other newspaper in the world".

But the Paris *Herald* was waxing strong to the detriment of the parent journal in New York. The man who actually runs a newspaper should be on the spot. Bennett was in Europe or cruising in tropical seas; his visits to New York were infrequent and almost furtive. Yet it was the edition in New York that supplied the bulk of his income. He strove to direct it by cable, even to indications for cartoons. But the European edition was foremost in his thoughts, and it was indeed a case of the tail wagging the dog. It could not work. Ever more jealous of his authority, Bennett in his declining years instituted a system of committees and boards – news committee, editorial committee, business board, board of control; committee piled upon board until in New York they numbered sixteen or eighteen, each sitting regularly in solemn conclave to prepare the paper for the next day, and each with a secretary drafting minutes of the meeting for the absentee owner. When he was cruising and his yacht called at some port for the mail, these minutes and those from Paris, where the committee system obtained also, would fill several bags. As each envelope bore an indication of the contents, Bennett would set aside all the minutes and, when he fancied he was not observed, motioned to the boatswain to heave the lot overboard. The system was sheer suicide so far as New York was concerned, with five, six or seven men taking five, six or seven times as long to recommend that something be done as it would have taken a managing editor to do it.

Innumerable stories were told of Bennett – and still are. Most of them are apocryphal. And in truth, as I found later, none of them reveals Bennett the man. Stories of the youthful days when he sowed his wild oats, of his carousings, of his love affairs, of his horses (later his automobiles), his dogs, his wilfulness, his summary dismissals. No wonder I hesitated. Yet one day, with John Parslow indicating the correct process, I wrote a letter to James Gordon Bennett, Esquire, asking for a position on the Paris *Herald*. It was winter and he was on his yacht. Eventually the reply came in the form of a telegram instructing me to report to the editor-in-charge at 38, Rue du Louvre, for a week's trial.

The telegram and the week's trial were typical of Bennett's ways. He telegraphed lavishly – for rapidity, he said. I always suspected two other reasons. One was ostentation. Some years later Bennett sent me to the Tyrol – characteristically enough, in midsummer to write on the next winter sports season! In Bozen (now Bolzano) I went to a hotel where he had himself stayed some months before. When I mentioned my connection with Bennett, the comment was: "Oh yes, the gentleman who sent so many telegrams! He must be very rich!"

97

The other reason was a dislike of letters. For despite governesses and private tutors he was not what one would call a well-educated man; truth to tell, he did not express himself with ease, either in conversation or in writing. He sent out much correspondence, of course, but seldom dictated: he indicated the general outline of letters which were then drafted for him.

As for the week's trial, that was his invariable rule; he paid the applicant, whether retained or not. In my case the Editor-in-Charge telegraphed to the yacht that I could fill his bill, and Bennett telegraphed back to engage me. So it was that on December 3, 1904, I began my career as an American newspaperman.

No. 38, Rue du Louvre had been a store. Putting ground glass in the windows was all that had been done to convert it into a newspaper office. In one large room toiled the editorial staff, a racial melting-pot in miniature. Perhaps half were American; the remainder English, Scot, Irish, French, Scandinavian – at one time there was even a Bulgarian. The tyro's first task was to assimilate *Herald* ways, to realise that the weather, automobiles, yachts, balloons, dogs, fox-hunting, grouse-shooting, fashions, art, antiques and the like were of more import than what is generally known as news. Bennett, with all his whims, was consistent in one thing: his paper was intended for Society, by which he understood the idle rich, interested primarily in means of passing their time and spending their money. That being so, our reference library consisted mainly of social registers, peerages and Almanachs de Gotha, to supplement which each man had before him a "taboo list". It set out the names of people never to be mentioned, either at their own request or at Bennett's order; of people to be mentioned only in specified circumstances (Princess Blank, for instance, wanted no reference to her Thursday at-homes); of people to be mentioned in the sports reports but not in the personal columns or vice-versa; of people who desired this, that or the other thing.

The newcomer learned also that Bennett was generally known as the Commodore, because at one time, many years before, he had been at the head of the New York Yacht Club. He was very proud of the fact, but he detested being styled "ex-Commodore". Doubtless that was the reason why he forbade the use in his papers of the designations "ex-king", "ex-president", and so forth. Having laid down the law: "Once a commodore, always a commodore" he had perforce to extend it to: "Once a king, always a king". The "taboo list" included also some other aversions, some sensible, others mere fads; he objected to "guests" at hotels, preferred "automobile" to "motor car" and would not hear of "planning" except by engineers and architects. In obituary notices he very properly insisted that the age of the deceased was a prime essential. As for news this is the sort of thing we printed:

"MOSCOW, Wednesday – The revolution here is a colossal swindle, engineered by a small number of manipulators, manufacturing terror with the criminal complicity of the sensational press. This I hope to prove." Whitman.

This, be it noted, was in December 1905, when Russia was becoming articulate and when the rising in Moscow was due as much to the "Black Hundred of Reaction" as to revolutionary terrorists.

For if Bennett, broadly speaking, was many things by turn and nothing for long, one thing he never was – a democrat. Himself dictatorial, he ever supported authority from whatever source it might derive. Naturally he sided with the Tsar, who moreover was a subscriber; each day a copy of the *Herald* was addressed to His Majesty the Emperor of all The Russias. He sided even with the Sultan of Turkey and the Shah of Persia.

His support of autocratic regimes had limits nevertheless – when they came into conflict with his own dictatorial views. The *Herald* was in the habit of reproducing cartoons from American papers. Once it reprinted from *Life* a strip showing what might become of some European crowned heads should they lose their thrones. Included among them was "Nicky Romanoff". As might have been expected, the strip was "caviared" at the Russian frontier. "Print it again every day for two weeks" ordered the Commodore, "and explain why, for the benefit of readers outside Russia. One or two copies may escape the censor's eye".

Bennett's outlook on Germany, however, was different – instinctively perhaps, for he had instinct. Naturally he admired Bismark. Once he had been received in audience by the Iron Chancellor. He referred to this often; one outward and visible reminder of the interview was truly Bennettian. Among his many idiosyncracies was the constant use of a blue pencil. When he did write a note it was in blue pencil; his signature to most letters was in blue pencil. The story goes that once he told a reporter that he would be remembered in his will (it was contained in an old leather bag which followed him everywhere) and, to convince him, brought out the document and amended it – in blue pencil. Those blue pencils were made specially; eighteen inches long, they bore the words: "Bismark blue".

But Bennett's admiration did not extend beyond Bismark. He invented a standing headline for all manifestations of Kaiser Wilhelm II's policy of expansion and pushfulness – "Those Terrible Germans!" A casino opened in Madeira with German capital – "Those Terrible Germans!" The Berlin-Bagdad Railroad scheme was discussed – "Those Terrible Germans!" At last word came that "high circles in Berlin" were not pleased. Bennett chuckled; "Those Terrible Germans!" appeared more frequently than ever.

An occasion presented itself when he might have used the largest possible type for that headline, but he changed his decision as quickly as he had made it. That was in 1911, when Wilhelm II sent a warship, the Panther, to Agadir Bay as a warning to France that he had something to say about Morocco. Bennett telephoned me to go to his house immediately. He seemed excited, pointed to a classified advertisement in the *Herald* of that morning and asked how long it would take me to get ready to go to Marseille with baggage for a trip of possibly several weeks. I answered: "Not more than an hour". That pleased him. "Good" he went on. "Here is what I want you to do. See this advertisement? It offers a German steam yacht for charter; she's a big boat and luxurious, now lying in Marseille. All the better for you. I'm going to charter this yacht and you'll represent me aboard. You'll take with you Gordon Smith to write despatches and also a photographer. But you will be the head of the expedition because you're French. From Marseille you'll make straight for Agadir Bay and drop anchor alongside the Panther. She's a German yacht flying the German flag so they'll let her come close. When they find that the charterer is a Frenchman accompanied by the correspondent of an American paper there'll be some fun. Cable fully whatever happens. Now go straight to the address indicated. The agent's office hours are from ten to noon."

There was an assignment indeed! It was 9.30. It did not take me many minutes to get to the man's office; it was in the Rue du Faubourg Saint-Honoré, I remember, a penthouse in the court. The door was locked. I waited impatiently for the clock to strike ten. No one appeared. I questioned the janitor, who remarked that it was quite unusual, for the man seldom failed to come to his office. I waited until 12.30, but in vain. After lunch I reported to Bennett, who said casually: "If he can't keep office hours, then he's no good". And that was the end of my Agadir adventure.

Another idiosyncracy was owls. The story went – the phrase recurs inevitably when dealing with Bennett; the story went that during the Civil War he commanded a gunboat and that when entering a bight on patrol duty, owls fluttering up from woods indicated the presence of Confederate craft. Be that as it may, the Commodore had adopted the bird. In the garden of his hunting lodge at Versailles there was a large live one in a cage. The others were carved of wood or cast in metal, in all sizes. They cluttered his desks. There were owls' heads in the pattern of his carpets, owls for interior decoration, owls everywhere. His stationary bore as crest an owl on a crescent moon; it was repeated on the olive-green livery of his domestics and on the doors of his automobiles. With the motto: "La nuit porte conseil", it was printed on the editorial page of the *Herald* for many years.

Two other traits should be mentioned. All letters criticising the editor or abusing him were invariably printed, sometimes in facsimile, and generally with sarcastic or humorous headlines. One, for example, contained this passage: "The *New York Herald* is NOT an American newspaper. IT IS A RICH MAN'S TOY and nothing else!" Secondly, his name was never mentioned in his own paper. So far as the *Herald* was concerned the various Gordon Bennett challenge cups for automobile, balloon or airplane contests became the "International Automobile Cup" and so forth. There was another characteristic; he refused all favours and expected his staff to do the same.

C. Inman Barnard, who died in Nice in May 1942 at the age of 92, dean of American newspapermen in Europe, learned this to his cost – but survived. While stationed in Cairo the Khedive of Egypt offered him a decoration. Barnard accepted the bauble. Bennett objected. Barnard insisted. The result was that they parted – and the *Herald* printed a vengeful editorial. It was neither news nor strictly ethical. Be that as it may, Bennett himself steadfastly declined to be decorated with the Legion of Honour, to a high dignity in which he could have aspired had he expressed the wish. Possibly he could afford to adopt that attitude; the fact stands nevertheless.

Yet once you knew the man and had appraised him it was possible to get along very well with Bennett – on condition that you possessed a sense of humour. When executives from New York were summoned to Paris they saw a Bennett who was playing a part. At bottom he was a shy man concealing shyness behind brusquerie; in the case of those with whom he was not familiar he was not his real self in conversation. It was different with those he met daily. Such was my case, for I was some twenty years with the *Paris Herald*, for the greater part of that time an executive or as near an executive as it was possible to be with the Commodore.

In May 1907 he had cabled from his yacht that I was to become Editor-in-Charge and some years later he removed me to the Rue du Louvre virtually to act as managing editor – but without that or any other title, of course. In the end I was vice-chairman of all the committees and boards – he naturally was chairman ex officio – and concerned myself with every department. Apart from the Editor-in-Charge no one had a title, which was normal since Bennett was everything, from editor to office boy. Often did he carry messages himself – in his car, it is true – from one of his many offices to another.

With this strong personality it followed that the very heart of the Paris *Herald*, and in some measure of the *New York Herald*, was where Bennett himself happened to be. The editing and the printing might be done Rue du Louvre, but the elaboration of the paper was done on the Champs-Elysées, where the Commodore was always supposed to be, even when cruising on his yacht. He was seldom there in the flesh, but he was ever there in spirit.

The story of Bennett's offices is as interesting as anything else pertaining to him. In his early days in Paris he had an apartment at 120, Avenue des Champs-Elysées. The rooms on the ground floor served as offices, with a special stairway leading to the flat above. When he removed to 104 on the same avenue into a larger apartment, he retained the offices at 120. And when he removed from 104 to a mansion on the Avenue d'Iéna, not only did he retain the whole of the apartment at 104 as offices but he did not part with 120. It was at 120, be it noted in passing, that Bennett was nearly killed when he insisted on driving his four-in-hand into the court. His head hit the top of the gateway and as he fell from his seat his abdomen was ripped open by the step of the coach.

This multiplicity of offices suited the Commodore perfectly. He was ever suspicious that things might be done with the *Herald* that he would not know. Consequently he isolated his executives as much as possible. So that at one time the *Herald* was directed by Bennett from his own residence on the Avenue d'Iéna and from his two offices on the Champs-Elysées, while the business office was on the Avenue de l'Opéra, the editorial office and the printing plant on the Rue du Louvre and the photographic department on the Rue Jean-Jacques Rousseau. There were several private telephone lines - very expensive and very erratic – linking these different addresses and also the hunting-lodge at Versailles. Several messengers did nothing else all day but carry notes and copy from one to the other. Frequently the Commodore's automobiles were pressed into service for this duty while he himself, with a grim smile, took the subway. But he was supremely happy with this arrangement – no one in his employ knew what the other was doing! Moreover, there was always the possibility that the Commodore himself might appear suddenly at one or other of the offices, if only to make sure that none dare call himself "The Editor".

For many years A.R. Hutt, former captain of Bennett's yacht, "sat in" at 120, with a page-boy in livery. A reader of the *Herald* would call: "Good morning. Are you the editor?" And Hutt would reply: "Oh dear no! I am a sailor. Mr Bennett is the editor". The reader would continue: "May I see Mr Bennett then?" Again the reply would come: "Oh dear no! Mr Bennett is cruising in the West Indies". The visitor might insist, whereupon he would be told that at 104, there "sat in" another man – myself, with a butler, a footman and a page-boy ready to wait upon the Commodore should he turn up unexpectedly – who might be of assistance.

The visitor would go from 120 to 104 where the conversation would be renewed on much the same lines "Oh dear no! I am not the editor. Mr Bennett is the editor. He is cruising in the West Indies". Quite possibly the upshot would be a cablegram to Bennett in the West Indies asking for instructions, then a cablegram from Bennett in the West Indies giving the instructions. Whereupon, if the matter concerned the publication of some item in the *Herald*, 104 would notify 120 and 120 would notify the Rue du Louvre, each of the three recording the notification on a daily report which went to the Commodore – to be read or to be cast overboard unopened.

That was the Commodore's theory of management. In practice it was different. The system was full of loopholes and nothing was easier than to take action and simply say nothing about it. The essential point was to send as many reports as possible, preferably on futile matters.

Not long before the First World War, Bennett was induced for motives of economy to abandon both 120 and 104 and to transfer everything to the Rue du Louvre. But such simplification was not to his taste. Not very many months later he had a new office on the Avenue d'Iéna facing his own house and under his very nose as it were.

Bennett did not read much, although of course he had a library of classics in rich bindings; he seemed to look upon them as a sort of interior decoration. It was open to doubt whether he had ever read Macaulay's Essays. Yet we discovered by chance that the volume opened invariably at a certain page of the essay on Frederick the Great. It included this passage:

"At Potsdam, his ordinary residence, he rose at three in summer and four in winter. A page soon appeared, with a large basket full of all the letters which had arrived for the King by the last courier ... He examined the seals with a keen eye, for he was never for a moment free from suspicion that some fraud might be practised on him. Then he read the letters, divided them into several packets ... By eight he had generally finished this part of his task. The adjutant-general was then in attendance, and received instructions ... In the meantime the four cabinet secretaries had been employed in answering the letters on which the King had that morning signified his will. These unhappy men were forced to work all the year round like black slaves in the time of the sugar-crop. They never had a holiday. They never knew what it was to dine. It was necessary that, before they stirred, they should finish the whole of their work. The King, always on his guard against treachery, took from the heap a handful of letters at random, and looked into them to see whether his instructions had been exactly followed."

If Bennett was not seeking to imitate Frederick, he must have been a sort of reincarnation, as the reader will be able to see. The part he played in the presence of those whom he summoned from New York was that of newspaper publisher and editor.

This part did not suit him, for it was impossible to separate Bennett the publisher and editor from Bennett the host of grand Dukes, in a word from Bennett in every other of his many roles.

Moreover the personal element was ever a factor in the instructions and the decisions of the Commodore, which instructions and decisions were impossible to understand by any one not in constant contact with him, familiar with his ways – and also with his language. For he had a wonderful knack of mixing things and his malapropisms would fill a volume. He loved to use homely proverbs and always quoted them wrong – "Keeping your nose to the milestone", for instance. If he made an unwanted incursion into the classics, he would speak of "Pericles who tied a tin can to his dog's tail". And he would mangle proper names until they were utterly unrecognisable, whether of acquaintances or of public figures. He would say "Juarez" for "Jaurès" and "saucisse" (sausage) for "sosie" (counterpart) so that when he discussed Juarez he was thinking of French politics, not of Mexico, and when he pointed to a photograph reproduced in the *New York Herald* with the remark that "Princess Blank is a sausage", he did not mean to be rude to the lady but merely that the person photographed was the very image of the princess.

If Bennett's conversation had been connected, the stranger perhaps might have made something of it. But it was not. It was terribly tangled, with interruption of every possible kind.

I would be at the office by eight o'clock. Bennett rose early and all his executives had to be on hand early also. The bell of the private telephone would ring. "Is that you?" came the Commodore's voice. He always said: "Is that you?" without mentioning your name. You guessed you were the man he wanted and replied: "Yes Mr Bennett." To which he rejoined: "Take a taxi, at my expense, and come here". That "at my expense" never failed.

107

On arriving at the house, the porter would telephone upstairs to ask into which room I should be ushered; if several men were summoned at about the same time, each one was made to wait in a separate room so that there might be no collusion. After a few minutes a servant would come to say: "Monsieur will see you in his dressing-room". In the dressing-room stood the Commodore, then in his sixties, a tall, gaunt figure in a bath-robe and rather forbidding, with large nose and steel-blue eyes full of suspicion. He stooped a little but threw his head back, possibly as a corrective.

Or it might be later in the day, when he was in his work-room. Always smart in dress though perhaps not always with taste, his trousers were invariably creased laterally, the reverse of the current practice – Edward VII had done so at one time. This gave a strange appearance to his long legs. But wherever it might be, the room was littered with newspapers, torn correspondence – and Pekingese dogs. He had to clear a chair for you, since every piece of furniture was covered with bundles of papers, each bundle representing the subject matter of conversation with a different visitor. He would take a bundle, look at it and put it back – again not the right one; then he would drop a bundle, retrieve it and lay it on another bundle; having thus mixed them, he would sort them out again, each one on a separate piece of furniture. Whereupon he realised that no chair had been cleared, and the game of bundle would be played once more. All the time you stood waiting.

Finally, when a chair was cleared, it might happen that he had forgotten that he had another engagement and I would go back to my office, to be asked some hours later to take another taxi "at my expense". Bennett was always forgetting something. Once, when he was at Versailles, he summoned by telegram both myself and the man who acted as business manager although he had not the title, with the indication that we would dine and sleep there. Incidentally luncheon or dinner

108

with the Commodore was somewhat of an ordeal, under the eyes of butler and footmen who seemed rather to scorn such business meals. Bennett was a rapid eater, and at the best it was not easy to keep pace with him. Also, he would press you with questions. While you answered in detail instead of eating, he would clear his plate, which fact was notice enough to the flunkeys to bring the next course. The cuisine was excellent, but you needed a sandwich afterwards all the same. After this particular dinner at Versailles he settled down to talk business, only to discover that he had left his papers in Paris and, in the absence of papers, had forgotten what he had to say.

If the Commodore had no other engagement, the conversation would proceed somewhat on these lines:

"Have you anything for me?"

"No, Mr Bennett". (If you had anything to tell him, it was wise to wait until the end of the interview; otherwise he was likely to forget what he had to tell you).

"I don't think that the make-up (of the Paris *Herald*) was very good this morning. Do you?"

"Well, Mr Bennett..."

"They could have put this here" (turning over the pages rapidly and pointing to one column after another), "and this here, and that there. That way they could have found room for a lot of things they left out."

"But wouldn't that still leave something out, Mr Bennett?"

"No, you don't understand. You put this here, and this here, and that there, and that there. Now do you see?"

"Oh yes, Mr Bennett" (anything for a quiet life).

"If they'd done that, they could have kept the apples with the apples and the pears with the pears. Like the 'Carneval de Venise' (a haberdashery store in Paris). "You know the Carneval de Venise, don't you?"

"Yes, Mr Bennett." (This is the hundredth time he has asked the question).

"Well, go and look in their windows. They keep the ties with the ties and the socks with the socks. Tell them at the Rue du Louvre to do the same. The apples with the apples."

"Yes, Mr Bennett."

Interruption. A page-boy comes in for the dogs. "Is it cold? No? Yes? Well, take them out but don't be long. And hold little black one on a leash." ---- To me: "Now look at this overset. Here's a report of Mrs Blank's dinner party and they haven't put it in."

"No, Mr Bennett!" (With an intonation intended to express the most extreme concern).

"No, they haven't. Yet I've told them a thousand times that society news is the bread and butter of the *Herald*. As I've told you before", (with an emphatic glare) "if the King of England and the German Emperor and the President of the Republic were all assassinated on the same day and the *Herald* didn't have a line about it, it wouldn't matter." (Mental comment from me: "I shouldn't like to be the man who left it out"). "The readers of the *Herald* would find it all in the *Gaulois* or the *Figaro* or the *Times* or *The Daily Telegraph*. But they can't find Mrs Blank's dinner party in the *Gaulois* or the *Figaro* or the *Times* or *The Daily Telegraph*. It's a beat. They must publish beats immediately."

"Yes, Mr Bennett."

Interruption. The chef enters to submit the menu for luncheon. "Hum! Hum! What's this? Sweetbreads? Yes. Hum! What's this? Strawberries? Why strawberries? (The chef is diffident). I don't want strawberries. Take them off." (The chef takes himself off too). --- To me: "Here's another piece of overset. It's a cockroach," (meaning an unusual story). "I've explained a hundred times that when you see a cockroach you should put it in. Tell them again."

"Yes, Mr Bennett."

"Now look at this in the unused copy." (The Commodore imagined that he had organised things in such a manner that everything came to his attention. Either copy was published and he saw it in the *Herald* or it was rejected and sent to him as unused copy, or it was crowded out and sent him in proof as overset. In practice much copy was made to disappear by sleight-of-hand. Otherwise those morning autopsies would have been unending. "Now look at this in the unused copy. It's from that man in Copenhagen, and it's about the King of Denmark. It should have been published at once. Tell them to publish it tomorrow. And remember: 'Obey orders, break owners!'"

"Yes, Mr Bennett."

Interruption. The page-boy returns with the dogs. "How far did you go?" --- To me: "And now here's something about Li-Sum-Ling." (Li was a Chinese newspaper man whom the Commodore had brought to America and then to Europe). "It must be published tomorrow. Let me explain I've sent Ohl (the late J.K. Ohl, who became managing editor of the *New York Herald* when it was bought by Frank A. Munsey), "to Peking at great expense and I've brought Li-Sum-Ling from Peking, also

111

at great expense. Now I want to get my money back by printing their articles. Ohl will tell about China from the American point of view, and Li-Sum-Ling will tell of America from the Chinese point of view. An American in China and a Chinese in America, each one telling about the other. It's an idea. You must have ideas. Jesus Christ had ideas. He was crucified."

"Yes, Mr Bennett." (But rather dubiously, because the meaning of all this is not very clear).

Interruption. The telephone rings. "Dead! Who's dead? Oh! How old was he? What did he die of? Yes. What do you say? Yes. Just what I had." (He hangs up the receiver). "It's Grand Duke Alexis. He died this morning". (A pause). "I knew it yesterday. No, I mean I knew it already." (As a newspaper publisher and editor, the Commodore felt that he must always know news before other people and his favourite exclamation was: "I knew it yesterday". This time it came tripping from his tongue before he realised what he was saying). "Have you anything for me?"

"Yes, Mr Bennett. Here is a card from Lord Blank. He's organising something on the Riviera and he asks the *Herald* to help him."

The Commodore takes the card, examines it on both sides, returns it and remarks: "What snobs these English! Yes help him. Anything else?"

"No, Mr Bennett."

"That's all then. I may send for you again this afternoon." (Calling after me) "Let me have that Lord's card". (As I go down the stairs I can hear the Commodore tell a servant: "Take this card and put it with the others on the silver tray in the salon").

Imagine what it must have been when Bennett outlined an editorial with similar interruptions and in the same disjointed manner. Imagine also how much a man would have understood who had not met him before. Yet Bennett made efforts to view journalistic matters with a detached mind. He strove hard to be Mrs Peabody. Mrs Peabody was a creation of his brain to represent the average reader or the man in the street. He would say: "Write for Mrs Peabody" and "Think of Mrs Peabody", and for a few minutes he would really imagine himself to be Mrs Peabody. But it could not last long and very soon Mrs Peabody made way for James Gordon Bennett.

It was Bennett and not Mrs Peabody who took two cows to assure a supply of fresh milk on the annual yacht cruise. It was Bennett who, in this connection, learned of tuberculosis in cattle and of the greater or lesser degree of resistance to the disease in certain breeds. It was Bennett who sent a reporter post haste throughout France to question veterinarians on the subject. And it was Bennett who ordered the interviews to be printed in Paris and to be cabled to New York for publication there also, column upon column. But it was poor Mrs Peabody who was expected to read it all.

It was Bennett and not Mrs Peabody who suddenly took interest in the relative merits of China tea and Ceylon tea. It was Bennett who ordered scores and scores of interviews on the subject in Europe and in America. But it was poor Mrs Peabody who was expected to read them.

Bennett's great failing, in short, was that while always invoking Mrs Peabody he ended by identifying her with himself. So that Mrs Peabody got only what Bennett desired. She got stories written for Bennett at Bennett's suggestion. She got stories written by Bennett's friends, not because they were good stories but because they came from friends. She got Bennett automobiles, Bennett dogs and Bennett yachts. For a time she did not get Theodore Roosevelt or William Randolph Hearst because Bennett had put their names on his "taboo list". She got Blank's dinner party even at the cost of not getting the simultaneous assassinations of the King of England, the German Emperor and the President of the French Republic.

In the long run the fare proved too rich for her digestion. The New York edition fell away. When Bennett died in 1918 it was declining fast. It was sold to Munsey by the executors in January 1920, together with the European edition, which was actually the greater asset at the time. Indeed, rumour had it that Munsey paid for it much less than the balance at the bank, for if the early years of the First World War had proved most difficult, the coming of the American Expeditionary Force had increased circulation tremendously. In May 1924 the *New York Herald* was merged into the *New York Tribune*, but the European edition maintained the old name for several years longer.

In Bennett's case the personal element was an asset to his newspaper – so long as it was kept within limits. That was precisely what he could not understand. The following example will show to what extent that personal element intruded itself and will serve to point the moral.

On his cruises the Commodore called at many out-of-the-way spots, Djibouti or Obock for instance. The arrival of his yacht was an event and the owner of the yacht was treated as a celebrity. He would improve the occasion by appointing correspondents in these places. They were all amateurs of course, and 99 per cent of their stuff went into the waste basket. But if Bennett got hold of it first it would be magnified into epoch-making news, because it was a "beat" he would say. Thus all I can recall of the man at Djibouti was that he would send Bennett a bag of coffee each New Year and once cabled that a new lighthouse on Cape Guardafui had begun to operate. The fact was of interest to mariners but scarcely to the average reader. Yet it was printed on the front page with large headlines – a "beat". Many of Bennett's beats, it must be confessed, were such only in the sense that other newspapers would ignore them deliberately.

Occasionally, of course, something really important would happen - a volcanic catastrophe or a shipwreck with great loss of life – and the *Herald* alone had a correspondent there. Then indeed it would beat the world.

The terrible thing was that the Commodore usually forgot to notify the Paris and New York offices of the appointment of these correspondents. He would tell them: "I have a personal telegraphic address which is 'Namouna, Paris' and I arrange things so that wherever I may be a telegram to that address is relayed automatically". He told this once to a man, a ship-chandler or something of the sort, he had appointed as correspondent at a small port on the Dalmatian coast. This appointment was not notified to either paper. The ship-chandler remained mute for many months. Then something happened.

The Commodore was cruising in the Indian Ocean. Out in Montenegro brigand bands began fighting. The ship-chandler saw his opportunity. The following telegrams were exchanged in consequence:

By wireless from Bennett on his yacht to the Paris office of the *Herald*: "Man in Dalmatia is telegraphing to 'Namouna, Paris' hundreds of words about brigand fights and they are relayed to me. Do other papers have anything about it? Is it a beat?"

Paris office to yacht: "Apparently nothing more than periodical petty clan squabble".

Yacht to Paris: "Man in Dalmatia still telegraphing. Tell him to send to Paris, not to me".

115

Paris to yacht: "Have no record here of Dalmatian correspondent's name or address".

Yacht to Paris: "For God's sake stop that man. He is still coming in".

Paris to yacht: "Have already telegraphed you no record that man here".

Yacht to Paris: "Man's name is so-and-so and his address so-and-so. Telegraph him urgent rates never send anything on any pretext in any circumstance."

CHAPTER 8

MEETING FOLK AND GOING PLACES

Interesting as it was, fascinating even, Bennett's personality did not advance my quest. He could not be considered a representative American and there was nothing democratic or even liberal about his two papers. But with the New Year in 1909 new duties afforded me greater opportunities. It was then that I was installed at 104, Avenue des Champs Elysées, in the largest room of a vast apartment filled with paintings of unusual proportions which Bennett had been induced to purchase and the sight of which he had come to loathe. One in particular, a life-size portrait of himself, he had relegated to a dark corridor, next door to the toilet. Even the fact that some of his beloved Pekingese figured on the canvas had not saved it from this humiliation. The portrait was by Henri Gervex, a friend of Bennett's. One day Gervex called at 104, the Commodore was out of town. Casually he asked: "What's been done with my portrait? I suppose it's been moved to the new house." I replied: "Oh no, it's still here. I'll show it to you." I did. Gervex gasped – and left abruptly.

My new duties were never defined clearly. On broad lines I served as link between Bennett and the Paris *Herald*. Another man, in another room, served as link between Bennett and the household. When the Commodore was in Paris I played possum. Sitting in splendid isolation in my large room I waited for him to appear or to send for me. When he was absent, either cruising or automobiling or staying at his villa at Beaulieu-sur-Mer on the Riviera, which meant six or seven months of the

117

year, I received all callers – the Great, Near-Great, Would-be-Great, or Great-to-be; cranks, faddists, spongers, beggars, crooks and what not, including occasionally some who had not even an axe to grind. It was not exacting work but it called for tact and diplomacy. You could do much with Bennett, you could even steer him in the direction you wished, but always on one condition – that you recognised that he alone was master and that you made it clear that everything you did was really done by him vicariously. It would never do to say to a caller: "I shall do what you ask". The correct formula was: "Mr Bennett's general instructions seem to cover your request and it will be attended to". And to make assurance doubly sure you wrote to James Gordon Bennett, Esquire, telling him what you had done in his name. Otherwise you laid yourself open to suspicion – and that was fatal. I know for a fact that in New York he set one executive to spy on another with instructions to report in code, in another case private detectives were hired. In Bennett's employment you were always dancing on a volcano. It was great fun nevertheless and full of excitement, for it was generally the unexpected that happened.

For that very reason it was well that Bennett's employees should have been young, for salaries also were erratic and budgeting for a family was out of the question. For instance, my promotion, if promotion it was, did not bring more money. That was not Bennett's system. The very day he returned from the first cruise during which I served as link, he came to 104, sat down and began writing a cheque. "How many months have I been away?" he queried. "Seven, isn't it?" And he wrote on while I said no: "No, Mr Bennett, only six". He turned round. "Never mind. Here's a cheque for 7,000 francs for the work you've done in my absence." But as years passed, sometimes there would be no cheque on his return. His idea was to keep you on a string, always expecting.

On the other hand, although cheques did not always come, exile was inevitable when he returned. It was a reminder, not only to you but to all the world, that you were not indispensable even though you had acted in his name for six months. Any pretext would serve. "I should like you to go to London and see the way they're running the office there." And to London I would go for four or five weeks. If he were well disposed I would be recalled by a telegram such as this: "Very pleased with your reports. You may return now. Go to my tailors and order yourself three suits of clothes at my expense." To be sent to his tailor was a token of the highest consideration – but your trousers were creased normally, not across like his. Sometimes the pretext for such periods of exile revealed his newspaper instinct. Thus in 1912 my mission was to study the collection and transmission of news in the event of a general European war.

My longest exile came at the end of 1913. Bennett was then in Biarritz. I had written to him on some business matter and in a moment of inattention had used the first person singular rather frequently. My letter came back with a note at the bottom – in Bismarck blue, of course – "I" (underscored three times) "shall attend to this on my return." Two days later a telegram instructed me to report on an aircraft display in the suburbs of Paris, a clear indication that I must not imagine that I was anything more than a reporter, mitigated nevertheless by placing one of his automobiles at my disposal for the day. I understood and was on my guard when he returned. For several weeks there was some amusing sword-play.

"How would you like to go to Egypt?" said the Commodore suddenly one afternoon. I realised that we were coming to the point and parried: "If you want me to go, Mr Bennett, I am at your orders". He went no further that day, the conversation ending as abruptly as it had begun. At intervals he put the question twice more in exactly the same words and got exactly the same reply. The fourth time the phrase changed to: "I want you to go to Egypt. When can you start?" My reply: "Whenever you like, Mr Bennett" showed him that he had won. Mollified, he outlined my mission. I was to arrange better distribution of the paper in Egypt and to coach the society correspondents. Obviously the pretext was flimsy, for our circulation was small there and the correspondents chronicled nothing more intricate than rounds of golf and dinner parties. Obviously also he held something up his sleeve. The date of my departure was fixed.

The morning of the appointed day he sent for me, repeated his instructions, said good-bye, shook hands limply, and wished me luck. My train left at night; he asked me to be at the office in the afternoon "in case he had anything more to tell me". He had. The telephone rang: "Is that you? You're going to have a little companion on your trip." He paused. (I was wondering: "A companion? What the devil does he mean? Is it a he or a she?") When he continued. "It's a dog, a little Pekingese dog I'm sending to Princess Izzet in Cairo, the wife of my friend Izzet Pasha, you know. A page-boy will meet you at the station tonight bringing the dog in a special travelling basket. Good-bye. Pleasant trip. Oh! I nearly forgot; the boy will give you written instructions for the dog's food."

To say that this left me speechless would be inexact; I cursed loud and long. So that was his game; out of the sleeve had come a Pekingese, expensive of course, delicate of course, and I was to be saddled with the creature from Paris to Cairo! The next thought was that two could play at that game. Forthwith I telephoned the sleeping-car people that I wanted two berths instead of one, "at Mr Bennett's expense" and I vowed that I would make him pay for all this – literally. Grinning from ear to ear, the boy duly brought the dog – it was a she, by the way. "Come to my car", I told him. "Now put her basket on the lower berth; I'll take the top. Pekingese are aristocrats, you know, and should be treated as such." He grinned all the more, but I had made my point. Bennett would question him, as was his wont. He could not but approve of my treatment of such a valuable animal – and would be prepared for some strange expense accounts yet to come.

My "companion" proved good-tempered and docile enough, but much too companionable. During the very first meal – I had left her in my cabin – a smirking steward came to the table to announce in an audible whisper: "Your dog is making an awful noise, Sir". I had to go and pacify her.

Wireless telegraphy was still in its infancy and expensive, which explained the smile on the operator's face when he handed me a message from Bennett: "Be very careful of the little dog on the promenade deck. She could slip overboard under the rails". That meant that I was restricted to the lower deck, unless I carried the animal. I wirelessed back: "Little dog quite safe. Am taking every precaution. Wind north. Thermometer 13". That last was a dig at him, intended to make it clear that although on the road to exile I was still his obedient servant. When the situation was reversed, I in Paris and he absent, one of my tasks was to cable him each day what he called a "news bulletin", always ending with meteorological data – direction of wind and temperature. Thereon hang my stories – as they invariably do with Bennett.

It will be no surprise that what he called "news bulletin" was nothing of the kind. In my candour I imagined at first that what he wanted was a summary of world events in the past twenty-four hours. I soon learned that what he desired was news, or rather gossip, about people he knew – this debutante was engaged, that man had influenza, and that sort of thing. It meant much research to ascertain his circle of acquaintance; in course of time I got to know most of them, chiefly by making mental notes of those mentioned in conversation. But

121

occasionally I would trip. One year an agency dispatch from Cairo reported the death of Izzet Pasha, the very man to whose wife I was taking my "companion" on this occasion. Naturally I led my "news bulletin" with the fact. Two days later came this: "Cannot understand your cable about Izzet. Am told he isn't dead." He wasn't. There were several Izzets in Egypt although I did not know it. "Which Izzet is it?" became a standing joke in the office.

As for the meteorological data; Bennett held a master mariner's certificate from the United States Government. Consequently he could boss his yacht just as he bossed his papers. But of course he must do the bossing in his own peculiar way. Not the barometer but the thermometer was his favourite instrument. In all his apartments and houses there were almost as many thermometers as owls – in every room, outside every window, in every corner of the gardens. It is even said of him that one night at sea he assured his navigating officer that, unable to sleep, he had worked out the position of the yacht – in blue pencil on the cuff of his pyjama coat – with the aid only of a thermometer and the stars he could see through the port-hole! Anyhow every telegram sent to him ended with the direction of the wind and the temperature.

To return to my "companion". It all ended by my carrying that dog in my arms everywhere I went on the ship. During the whole of my stay in Egypt – the exile lasted four months – and even years later, people would say to me: "Surely, we have met before. Oh yes, I remember. You're the man who was on board the Prinz Regent Luitpold carrying a little dog." The boat called at Naples for half a day; I could not go ashore because I should have had to take the dog along. I was at the rail watching passengers going off sightseeing when the ship's doctor came by my side. He looked at the animal in my arms and said: "Why, that dog's got mange!" That was the climax.

Until we reached Alexandria it was medicines, ointments, salves, washes, dips. My cabin was a hospital, my life a misery.

From Alexandria I should have liked to go straight to Cairo to rid myself of the incubus. But I had to look into the circulation of the *Herald*, although we did not sell more than two score copies there; fortunately there was no correspondent to coach. Finally, two days later, I drove to Shepheard's Hotel in Cairo, carrying the Pekingese in her basket. The hall porter was officious. "No", I said firmly, "I do not want to see my room. No, I do not want anything to eat or drink. What I do want, and that immediately, is a cabman to take me in a swift carriage to the palace of Izzet Pasha. And let there be no mistake. You know Mr Gordon Bennett, don't you? Well the Izzet I want is Mr Gordon Bennett's Izzet. Understand?" He understood. Twenty minutes later I was dog-less. The Pasha regretted that I could not deliver the present personally to the Princess. "But in the East, you know, our women live rather secluded." I preferred it that way; it was swifter. A cup of Turkish coffee, a cigarette, and I drove off – a free man. It happened to be Christmas Eve.

Back at Shepheard's I cabled Bennett: "Arrived Cairo. Delivered little dog. Wind South. Temperature 32". Then I had a bath, a high-ball and my revenge. I sat down and wrote:

EXPENSE ACCOUNT – December 18-24

(1) For Little Dog

Dec.18 Tip to sleeping-car porter for various services 20francs

Dec.19 Tip to steward for attending to dog	10 francs
Tip to chef for special food	10 francs

Dec.20 Tip to steward	10 francs

Etc ….. etc….etc

(2) For Self

Incidental expenses on board   5 francs

      We were not supposed to charge gratuities and the like but no questions were ever raised about that account.

      I passed three weeks in Cairo, saw the booksellers who distributed the *Herald,* made the acquaintance of our correspondent, arranged for the paper to be available on Nile steamers, telegraphed occasional "news" - ("Many well-known people left for Upper Egypt by tonight's train. They include the Duke of So-and-so, Mr John Blank of New York, etc…etc…") - and set out to see Cairene life. Then, supposing my mission ended, I cabled Bennett to that effect. The reply was: "Do the same at Luxor". A week there, another cable: "Go on to Aswan". A week there, another cable: "Go to Khartoum". By that time I no longer cared. He could have sent me by easy stages to the Cape if he had wished. There was really no work for me to do but see the sights, meet interesting people – and spend his money.

      At Khartoum I began to understand. The Commodore's party that winter's cruise wished to hunt big game and I was to prospect possibilities and prepare the trip. Incidentally Bennett's shoots at Versailles were famous. He had rented from the French Government a delightful lodge, La Lanterne, dating from Louis XV. There he entertained in princely style and the bags were always large, for the very good reason that before each shoot thousands of partridges and hundreds of pheasants were brought from Hungary and other parts of Central Europe.

So Egypt had been chosen as my place of exile because of the hunting expeditions and also because of the little Pekingese dog. As he might have malapropped it, he was "hitting two stones with one bird". I entered into the spirit of the thing and decided to lead the life of a man of leisure until he saw fit to recall me. After an insight into the Anglo-Egyptian Sudan, I divided my time between Cairo, Aswan and Luxor, daily enlarged my circle of acquaintance, entertained and was entertained, dabbled in archaeology and was beginning to become a local figure when there came a telegram from Bennett announcing the passage of his yacht at Port Said and asking me to meet him there.

He received me cordially enough, but really we had very little to say. Moreover I was on my guard. Had I manifested a desire to return to Paris, he would certainly have found a pretext to send me elsewhere. So I enlarged on the pleasant time I was having in Egypt and the delightful country it was. As for business, I merely repeated the gist of the reports I had been sending him at intervals. Then came the moment for him to take a decision.

"Have you anything else to tell me?" he asked. I replied that I needed money.

"But", he countered, "I sent you a cheque only last week. You seem to have been spending a lot."

"I have, Mr Bennett. But it can scarcely be otherwise. It was you who told me to go to Shepheard's and it was you who told me to introduce myself as acting on your behalf. That means they've been making me pay everywhere on the scale they charge you."

He reflected. Then: "Hum! You can go back to Paris when you like. Goodbye."

125

I took the first train to Cairo. A boat sailed the next day for Marseille, but every cabin was reserved. Invoking Bennett's name, I succeeded in obtaining an assistant purser's bunk and the return trip began – this time without a "companion". Nothing prevented me from seeing Naples; then two days roaming about Marseille. I had learned my lesson. In Paris I cabled Bennett: "Arrived Paris. Await your instructions. Wind South-East. Thermometer 29." No reply. A week later I cabled anew. Again no reply. A third cable had no more result.

Then came news, indirectly, that the Commodore was lying very sick at Port Sudan, with pneumonia threatening. It appeared that one night, during a storm, he had insisted on going on the bridge in his pyjamas to take charge of navigation. This explained his silence but did not alter my policy. I continued to wait, did no work beyond calling at the office each day to see if perchance instructions had arrived – and each weekend drew my salary. Six weeks later, at the end of April, Bennett cabled: "Surprised at absence your name from minutes of committee meetings. How's that?" I replied that I had sent three messages, citing texts and dates, and adding: "Pending your instructions would not have presumed assume any duties". He cabled back: "Your cables must have come while I was sick. Wish you resume all your former work."

By the time the cruise ended the international situation in Europe had clouded, and each week grew worse. But Bennett had made up his mind there could not be war "just for a few Serbs". In July his chief concern was a "contest in make-up" he had devised. Several of his executives, including myself, were to be responsible for bringing out the *Herald* for a period of two weeks each. The work adjudged best would be rewarded with a gold watch, suitably inscribed. Everyone spoke of war, but he was absorbed in his new pastime. He bought the watch, displayed it to all and sundry and thought of nothing else. By the time the contest ended I was mobilised and at the front. My colleagues, all above military age or non-belligerents, suggested that in the circumstances it would be a nice gesture to award me the watch. Bennett would not hear of it. The upshot was that he took the watch down to Beaulieu-sur-Mer; a burglar broke into the villa and included it in his loot.

Ever consistent in his inconsistency, Bennett had arranged a trip by road to Carlsbad with a party of friends from America. Having decided to his own satisfaction that there would be no war, nothing would induce him to modify his plans. He left Paris three days before the opening of hostilities – and got no further than Nancy. Nor was it easy for him to return, what with troop movements and martial law. He was telegraphing me and I was telegraphing him, but to no avail since transmissions were delayed indefinitely, the lines being congested with official messages.

On Saturday, August 1, 1914, general mobilisation for France was proclaimed at 3.30 pm. The *Herald's* editorial committee met as usual at four, under my presidency. The situation was tense. I was due to join my infantry regiment on the Monday morning. Bennett was still in parts unknown. I suggested a number of steps to be taken immediately – contact with the military authority, orders for as much newsprint as was available, and the like. I did not hesitate to take authority which in normal times might have meant immediate dismissal, and I did it openly, with full mention in the minutes.

Early next day, Sunday, I was at the office. For once it was I who was calling Bennett on his private telephone. The janitor said: "Yes, Monsieur returned late last night, but I do not know whether he will see you!" My reply was: "Tell Mr Bennett from me that certain things have happened since yesterday and I for one join up tomorrow. I am not asking whether he can see me; tell him I'm coming along to see him." Two minutes later the man telephoned: "Monsieur will see you immediately".

I took a taxi – not at his expense for a change, since I never had another occasion to put in an expense account – and found Bennett rather abashed that war should have come after all. I told him what I had done and made some more suggestions. He approved and held out his hand to grasp mine. But I spoke: "There is something more, Mr Bennett. You have in your employ a number of Frenchmen who are off to the war. Most of them occupy modest posts. They are worried about their families. Some of them were waiting for me this morning. They want to know what you are going to do." The Commodore, give him credit, rose to the occasion: "I shall pay them half salary for the duration of the war". I am sure he meant it; we all imagined that the campaign would be short. He continued payment for one year, then ceased, save in my case. He wrote me at the front a very considerate letter – in blue pencil – saying that I would remain on half-pay to the end. He died in May 1918 at the age of 78; the *Herald* honoured his word to me.

I saw him but once again, when leave from the front was initiated in the spring of 1915. I had been wounded and given the Croix de Guerre. He was very cordial but seemed ageing. He was true to type to the last. Fingering the medal on my coat, he remarked: "So that's the Croix de Fer" (German Iron Cross!)

The reader may find these reminiscences very discursive. How could they be otherwise, dealing with such a man? When I look back upon my association with him, it is in a forgiving spirit. He was a hard master, an eccentric egotist, but his very eccentricities had their attraction. Above all, he had a strong, well-defined personality, which fitted with my inborn revolt against conformism. I have no harsh words for Bennett; working for him was a constant battle, but victory was not always on his side, despite the odds – and the fighting sharpened one's wits. Nor can I forget that thanks to him, although it certainly was not his design, I had unusual opportunities of seeing things and studying men.

That trip to Egypt, for instance. I met there Lord Kitchener, who under the modest title of His Britannic Majesty's Agent and Consul-General in Cairo virtually governed the country. Taciturn and wilful, his trend was towards personal rule; yet a few months earlier he had suggested to the Khedive the advisability of granting a parliamentary constitution on as democratic a basis as was compatible with conditions then existing. He did much for the numerous peasant class and curbed the greed of usurers. "K of K" could be affable on occasion, but always the "grand seigneur".

There was another potent figure in Egypt then, plain George Harrison, Head of Thomas Cook (Egypt) Ltd, as much in his way the uncrowned King of Egypt as Kitchener was in his. The tourists he brought to the country contributed in no small measure to its prosperity. Typically English, pink-cheeked and grey-haired, portly and gouty, benign but firm, he viewed Egypt in terms of special trains, tourist steamers, dahabiehs, dragomans and personally conducted trips. In Shepheard's bar, gathering-place of a very mixed cosmopolitan crowd, there was George Harrison's table. There was to be met, for one, Léon Carton de Wiart, noted Belgian jurisconsult; his son became a British general who played a part in both wars – one eye, one hand and the Victoria Cross. There were also Britons, French, German Swiss, an occasional American, native officials (one mudir, or provincial governor, had been at Oxford University), lawyers, doctors, soldiers, bankers, hotel men and what not. Much of the talk recalled the land boom of some years before, which had brought large fortunes to many venturers then living in veritable palaces on the banks of the Nile. These men formed a dominant class and they were anything but democratic.

Possibly it was in Cairo that conceptions of democracy began to modify themselves in my mind. If the native press correctly reflected the native mind, the national demand was for liberty in the abstract sense and, above all things, the right to vote. In the natural course of things this demand was strongly supported by the Liberals in England who considered a parliamentary regime as the political panacea. This might suit the wealthy class in Egypt and the students, but when one mixed with the fellaheen in their villages it became evident that personal liberties and social reform regardless of who granted them, were much more important than elections and political bosses.

One other person I remember well because of a certain conversation. The manager of Shepheard's was a young German from Wurttemberg – very suave, very efficient, perhaps over-polite to a Frenchman. We became friendly. He had a powerboat on the Nile, rather a rarity in those days; he would lend it to friends for picnics. Sitting one day in his office, he showed me a photograph of himself in military uniform. "I am a Reserve Officer in the artillery", he explained. "I am as fond of riding as I am of the river. I can satisfy both tastes by lending my boat to British officers, who in return let me ride their horses. Last week I spent a very pleasant day following manoeuvres near the Pyramids. They also invite me occasionally to their mess." I marvelled at the time at the easy going ways of British officers. Later, when under German leadership, the Turks attacked the Suez Canal, I wondered whether German residents in Egypt had not furnished preliminary surveys to the General Staff in Berlin.

I met Americans, too, in Egypt and Sudan – from all parts of the United States – archeologists, medical missionaries, business men on vacation and tourists on round-the-world trips. It was my first introduction to Americans in the mass, but already I discerned some national traits, accentuated or attenuated in later years – affability, hospitality, gregariousness, a devouring thirst for information, candour verging on puerility, ingrained nationalism entailing a certain measure of insularity – and, in the view of a Frenchman, queer tastes in food. Most striking of all perhaps was the contrast between French diffidence in the presence of strangers and American informality.

I had not found these characteristics so pronounced among Americans working for the *Herald*, no doubt because the majority had been in Europe some time. Instances of provincialism or insularity were provided however when Bennett brought over some executive from New York, generally to make it clear that he was not indispensable, since he could be kept in Paris indefinitely while his work was being done by someone else on the other side. What impressed me in most of these men was that they could see no further than New York, or rather that they imagined that New York was synonymous with the universe. Incidentally, my experience is that New Yorkers may prove the most insular and provincial of all Americans.

I recall one conversation. "Why don't you display your chief news of the day as we do in New York?" said one of these periodic visitors. "The outside right-hand columns are our best and that's where we put our hottest news."

"Why?" I asked

"Because on the newsstands the papers lie folded in four and the right-hand columns are apparent."

"A very good reason. But here in France the newsvendors fold their papers so small that only the title of the sheet is apparent, so it does not very much matter whether we display our news on the left or the right."

"Oh, I didn't know that."

One revelation, however was quite disturbing – the matter of liquor.

The majority of my fellow workers were moderate drinkers, even abstainers, but some seemed bent on maintaining the fast-disappearing tradition that a newspaper man must be an old soak. They would keep steady for weeks, then disappear from circulation for several days or be brought to the office in a cab by policemen who had found them prone in the gutter, or wanting to throw themselves into the Seine, or more frequently picking quarrels in the street. Fortunately for them their salaries precluded many carouses a year. I had already noted the effects of alcohol in a more prosperous sphere. On the way to Egypt I had made the acquaintance of a wealthy lumberman from the Middle West who had arranged a dinner party at Shepheard's for New Year's Eve; everything was of the best, but our host was absent, incapable of receiving his guests.

At first I ascribed these lapses to weakness of character. Yet the majority of these men, as I learned later, were able to reform and become either abstainers or moderate drinkers. If they could show firmness of character then, why not before? Moreover it was not the average quantity of liquor they consumed over a month or a year that was extraordinary. No doubt many Frenchmen drank as much or more. The surprise was the concentration of their craving into periodical bouts.

Contrasts such as these were facilitated in my case by the variety of people I would see when Bennett was absent. The Europeans for the most part were contributors or would-be contributors to the *Herald*. The Americans for the most part were expatriates. First in the former category were penurious titled folk who supplied society paragraphs – princes, viscounts, barons. They were more interested than interesting. There were also writers of many kinds, including members of the French Academy – Paul Bourget, who had remained very bourgeois in spite of his success with the aristocracy, and Anatole France, the secret of whose limpid prose was to be found in his proof-sheets, corrected again and again until the foreman printer tore out his hair. They wrote tales for the Christmas and Easter numbers. There was Camille Flammarion, the *Herald's* "tame astronomer", whose part it was to bring science within the comprehension of the idle rich. In Bennett's absence once we had printed articles by another astronomer. Orders came to cease. On his return the Commodore explained: "When Flammarion wanted to build his own observatory he touched me for a fair sum. Now I'm getting my money back." There was Professor Albert Robin, Bennett's doctor, who also edited the book page; he was very popular among society hostesses, many of whom were his patients; he used to call Bennett "Cher maître". And Bennett loved it.

There were also the people I was sent to see, especially in varied French newspaper circles. The *Herald* had friendly relations with two in particular, the *Figaro* and the *Matin*. Gaston Calmette was then editing the former, which still maintained that boulevard tone which had made its reputation. A charming man, he would generally gratify Bennett's whims by reproducing from the *Herald* items to which he attached importance. One day in 1905 even courteous Calmette gasped when asked to reprint an editorial violently attacking Théophile Delcassé, that Foreign Minister who had brought about the Entente Cordiale with Britain. Bennett seldom intervened in French politics; this time he had done so with a vengeance. Calmette did as he was asked, but felt constrained to tell his readers: "It goes without saying that the *Figaro* does not publish as its own all the ideas, and especially the way in which they are expressed in the *Herald*". It is related of Villemessant, who founded the Figaro, that a friend found him one morning rubbing his hands with satisfaction. "Excellent paper this morning", he said. The friend remarked that he saw nothing extraordinary in the news. "Perhaps not", came the reply, "but every line in the paper has been paid for". We of the *Herald* wondered how much it had cost Bennett that day.

There were other celebrities, more than one of whom mixed in American circles in Paris and imagined that these faithfully reflected America. They were hopelessly wrong. To explain why calls for consideration of the expatriate. But before leaving Bennett there are still other figures to depict, among them three men who became Prime Ministers.

CHAPTER 9

FOUR PREMIERS

Towering above all the figures to be met at Bennett's parties was Georges Clemenceau, veteran of a hundred political battles, the man who made and unmade cabinets, whose biting wit and ferocity in debate had won him the name of "The Tiger"; the man who, when the situation was at its darkest in the winter of 1917 was swept into office by sheer force of public opinion, grasped the helm with a strong hand, sent traitors before the firing squad, reduced defeatists to impotence and galvanised the nation into winning the First World War – "Le Père la Victoire" ("Old Man Victory"). A good shot, he frequently attended Bennett's hunts at Versailles. All enjoyed his sarcastic sallies, which spared none; even his butts smiled, though wryly.

In those days Clemenceau was nearing seventy but still full of vigour – masterful, wilful, pugnacious, ever ready to lash out, brave both morally and physically. In a career which had switched from medicine to politics, he had long been satisfied to remain a wrecker of ministries and had reached the age of sixty-five before taking office for the first time. He began as Minister of the Interior, soon thereafter to become Premier for three consecutive years – a long spell in France. Strangely enough for one destined to live in history as leader of a nation in war, one of Clemenceau's early steps was to curb the Army. He amended one of Napoleon's decrees so as to give precedence at each rung of the official ladder to the civil authority over the military. So, too, as long as the war lasted he upheld Foch and defended him against all comers. But immediately after the Armistice he humiliated the commander of the Allied and Associated Armies – never before had one man headed such a host – by bluntly telling him that his task was ended and that he had no part to play in drafting the peace treaty. Yet twenty years later Foch's prophetic words stood out: "When you are master of the Rhine you are master of Germany. When you are not on the Rhine, all is lost".

Clemenceau's attitude finds explanation in the fact that to the last he was a Jacobin and as such was suspicious of possible military coups. In the "eighties" of the last century he had had one experience – with General Boulanger, whom he had considered a republican and had imposed on the then Premier as Minister of War, only to realise later that his protégé had ambitions as dictator. But if Clemenceau was a Jacobin it does not follow that he was a democrat. As a politician he advocated freedom of speech, as a journalist he advocated freedom of the press, but he was too masterful to concede many liberties to others.

In 1914, for instance, when in the background as a mere senator and editor who on occasion bitterly criticised the government, Clemenceau had protested signally against censorship by changing the name of his newspaper: from *The Free Man* it had become *The Man in Chains*. Yet when he returned to power his instructions to censors were severer than at any time before, and what is more he prolonged the system during the whole of the Peace Conference. One of his orders: "Nothing may be printed against Woodrow Wilson", was applied with such rigour that Franco-American relations suffered the effects for years.

Georges Mandel was then Clemenceau's "chef de cabinet". Long associated with "The Tiger" in subordinate positions, he had been the target of many harsh outbursts from his chief. (Clemenceau used to say: "Quand je pète, c'est Mandel qui pue"). But Mandel was the kind of man to accept all rebuffs and bide his time, confident that when the chief came to the fore again he would have a place of authority. He did – and not without reason was accused of using that authority tyrannically. In after years Mandel was elected to the Chamber of Deputies and in due course elevated to the Cabinet. At every stage of his ministerial career the accusation of tyranny was renewed. In the end he was arrested in Morocco after the French defeat in June 1940, charged with attempting to overthrow the government with British connivance.

Some made of him a hero; others derided, chiefly because of his race – he is a Jew. History may show him in his true light. Certainly France never had such an efficient Postmaster-General, but certainly also he too frequently proved intolerant and vindictive. Refusing allegiance to any party, he played a lone hand, filed everything that could serve against his opponents – and much enjoyed the sweets of power.

Be that as it may, as Clemenceau's "chef de cabinet" Mandel controlled the censors and his rule was to interpret instructions in the most limitative sense. So it was in the case of Wilson. Apart from jurists – and not all of these – the French had hazy notions of the Constitution of the United States. They assumed that if the President had come to Europe, this very fact implied plenary powers; they little expected that the Senate would have its say. Thanks to Mandel, whenever press despatches from New York or Washington suggested opposition to Wilson, actual or latent, the censor denied publication – "Nothing against Wilson". And the French remained in blissful ignorance.

Thus it came about that when the Senate refused to ratify the Peace Treaty, even to accept the League of Nations, opinion in France utterly failed to understand. Many considered that they had been hoodwinked, which feeling long endured. It had not abated by the time war debts became a serious issue and served further to complicate relations. Clemenceau himself, for that matter, was not much better informed. Moreover, he had his own conception of the United States. In his youth he had gone there as to a land of opportunity, but evidently found none for himself, although he did bring back a bride. Nor, judging by his comments in later life, had he discovered there a form of democracy which appealed to him. By 1919 he had not learned much more of America, towards which he was too prone to adopt the attitude of a cynical and blasé European, much amused by Wilson's candour. To complete the picture it should be added that Clemenceau was a Voltairian agnostic.

Delightful in conversation, Clemenceau would tell with glee at Bennett's hunting luncheons of his initial day as Minister of the Interior. Ever an early riser, he was the first on duty, only to discover that officials arrived late – all the later in proportion to their rank. So he posted himself at the foot of the stairs, noting names and times as the astonished personnel filed past. He always liked a joke. On his first visit to police headquarters, he began an address thus: "Here I stand, the first cop of France!"

Clemenceau was not a democrat. He was essentially a product of the French Revolution, as sufficiently explained by the fact that he had been born only fifty years after that great upheaval. The Revolution was the work of the bourgeoisie – and he was a bourgeois. Clemenceau and his school of thought accepted the Revolution as a dogma; he himself insisted that it was "a block from which nothing can be removed". Today, with clearer perspective it is conceded by all unbiased thinkers that the Revolution had as many faults as it had qualities, a description by the way which fits Clemenceau himself. The Revolution is replete with paradoxes. One of them is that the doctrine enunciated in 1789 permitted the development of that economic liberalism – capitalism if you will – which a century and a half later tended to be superseded by state socialism, a concept which the French Constituent Assembly had rejected with horror. And today it is clear that one of the tasks of the peacemakers-to-be will be to decide whether capitalism really is obsolete.

In 1919, at the Peace conference over which he presided, Clemenceau found himself in ideological conflict with both Lloyd George and Woodrow Wilson, whose outlooks were very similar in many respects. On one point in particular, the left bank of the Rhine which Foch so ardently wanted for France, he could obtain no more than two defensive treaties, one with Britain, the other with the United States. Both countries pledged themselves to come to the aid of France in case of unprovoked aggression by Germany within the next ten years. But Britain made her ratification dependent on that of the United Sates. As Washington declined to ratify, the two treaties became nugatory.

This and other setbacks eventually sapped much of The Tiger's prestige, if not his popularity. So long as the country was at war, his virtual dictatorship had been accepted as inevitable as well as desirable, but Parliament never forgave him for having excluded it from some sort of participation in the peace negotiations, even if only in a consultative capacity. The Left even taxed him with "militarism". When Raymond Poincaré completed his seven-year term as President of the Republic, Clemenceau – though he disdained to stand as candidate – would have considered the post as the crowning of his career. Paul Deschanel was elected instead, and The Tiger retired to his lair on the coast of Vendée, embittered and solitary, until he died.

The Rhine question had brought "militarist" Clemenceau into conflict with a man as wilful and masterful as himself – General Charles Mangin, one of the most remarkable

139

figures of the First World War. His exploits in Africa for some twenty years had made him famous; his driving power in the field was unexcelled. No mean writer, a lover of music, he was brilliant in all he undertook. After the Armistice he commanded the French forces of occupation; behind the scenes he favoured the creation of an independent Rhenish Republic. To this both Woodrow Wilson and Lloyd George strenuously objected and Clemenceau had to recall Mangin, who died suddenly in 1925. My last glimpse of him afforded a typical picture of the man. In full parade uniform, wearing his many decorations, accompanied by his wife and several of his children, he was walking across Paris to a suburban cemetery behind the hearse bearing the body of his Senegalese batman. Had Mangin had his way, had there been a buffer state on the Rhine, the future course of Germany – and of the world – might have been different.

Clemenceau represented a political generation which was fast passing away. In dress, in manner, in oratory even, he was being outmoded. Whenever he proposed to make a set speech he observed the old custom of appearing in the Chamber in frock-coat and top hat. In demeanour, too, he remained old-fashioned and he would not accept the easy familiarity between representatives of the people, regardless of party, which was then developing in the lobbies and which contributed to making politics a profession if not a limited corporation. In delivery, although always decisive, he did not scorn occasional flowery passages. Therein he was reminiscent of the Revolution.

At heart Clemenceau was an aristocrat. It is doubtful whether universal suffrage appealed to him, especially after his absence from Parliament for some ten years when the electorate was swayed by a campaign accusing him of being "in the way of England". As a politician he well knew the value of votes; possibly he saw in them only a means to an end. In any case one of his famous pronouncements was made on the eve of a presidential election. After discussing the merits – and demerits – of the diverse candidates he summed it up: "I'll vote for the dumbest".

André Tardieu, Clemenceau's disciple, represented another generation. Brilliant at college, generally taking first place in competitive examinations, he had not yet entered politics when I first knew him, but was making a reputation as a journalist specialising in foreign questions. For Bennett he wrote articles to be cabled to New York. Not long thereafter he was elected to the Chamber of Deputies and it became manifest that it would not be many years before he reached Cabinet rank.

But the First World War intervened. At the outset Tardieu was press attaché on Joffre's staff. Soon he applied for an active command and fought at Verdun as captain of Chasseurs. Then he was sent to the United States as High Commissioner, to arrange for purchases of material and generally to pave the way for cooperation.

In this connection I must recall a personal incident which may throw light on the extent to which the Third Republic had become a regime of unbridled appetites. I had served some thirty months at the front, been wounded, and the Croix de Guerre had been pinned on my chest at a parade on the glacis of Fort du Regret at Verdun to the accompaniment of booming cannon. I felt no compunction, therefore, in writing to Tardieu, recalling our acquaintance-ship and suggesting that I might serve him usefully in his relations with the American press. He replied cordially but negatively. The gist was: "Yes, I appreciate fully, but what can I do? Already I have scores of applications for the position you suggest, each one endorsed by several Senators and Deputies. Sorry! Put yourself in my place." I remained in mine. But I understood. Patronage! The curse of every form of government.

Certainly patronage helped to compass the fall of France. On June 22, 1940, under the emotion provoked by news of the Armistice, I cabled from Bordeaux to the *New York Times* a despatch ("Take Heed America") in the form of an imaginary interview with a French peasant, wise with years and introspective. Later I learned that it had been read into the *Congressional Record* and reprinted in 1941 as a brochure by a post of the American Legion to commemorate Armistice Day. There is not one word to change today.

Said my mouthpiece in part: "We have lacked an ideal. I confess that in this matter I have been as guilty as most of my countrymen. We came to imagine that the proper duty of men was to arrange an easy way of life, individualistic to the point of selfishness.

We followed the wrong road. We all were democratic in spirit but in reality we were too much concerned with self. It was to a great extent the fault of our institutions, which tended to breed politicians instead of statesmen and which set party interests before those of the nation.

We saw no further than the parish pump and we were well satisfied when our representatives in Parliament brought home some of the gravy. We looked upon the State as a universal purveyor and we always spoke of our dues, seldom of our duties.

To tell the truth all parties are equally responsible. All of us, in every party, look upon our representatives as natural intermediaries between ourselves and the government for the distribution of manna from the State coffers.

We persisted in our errors. For one thing we persisted in levelling the nation down and in imagining that the State would prove an everlasting milch cow.

Tell all this to the Americans and warn them at the same time of the perils that may befall democracy everywhere when it forgets that free men have duties as well as rights."

Tardieu, to revert to him, might have written in that strain in his later – and disabused – years. At that time, however, he imagined that he could compel events. Yet he was not very successful in his American mission. For he also had preconceived notions. His intellect was of a classic mould, which reflected on his methods even in business deals. When he returned to France, Clemenceau made full use of his talents in the preparation of memoranda for the Peace Conference and also in drafting many of the articles of the Treaty of Versailles.

In such tasks Tardieu exemplified to the highest degree a trend which contributed to create a mentality explaining in some measure defeat and the apathy that accompanied it. For decades the end of education in France had been superficial brilliancy, ever analytical. The system professed to be Cartesian, but in reality it was only a parody. At school, at college, in their eventual professions, Tardieu and his fellows could write remarkable essays on any subject, but all made to measure as it were. Tardieu's own précis marshalling French claims to the left bank of the Rhine was masterly – as rhetoric and special pleading. From the archives of the Quai d'Orsay it may find its way someday into anthologies. But in 1919 it led to nothing. Prosaic Lloyd George and Woodrow Wilson were not impressed. Not that they disdained words, the "Welsh Wizard" especially, but they had their own use for them.

Soon Tardieu became Prime Minister for the first time. Among the members of his cabinet was Pierre Laval. For the next five or six years the then famous Tardieu-Laval "tandem" directed the destinies of the country. The two men presented a great contrast. Tardieu, of good bourgeois stock, very ambitious, fully aware of his intellectual superiority never hesitated to display his talents. In statesmanship he remained a disciple of Clemenceau – and as headstrong as his master. Nor was he animated by very pronounced democratic ideals. In political hue he was a Moderate; his conception of government was that it should rest in the hands of an elite, in which naturally a prominent place was reserved for himself.

Very soon he became adept at the parliamentary game. He had assimilated the technique so well that he shone even in such drab posts as Minister of Agriculture or of Public Works. But he realised in due time that whoever won at this game the country was always a loser. Statesmanship was impossible when leaders, in order to remain in office, were compelled to ward off daily attacks made on the flimsiest pretext or on no pretext whatsoever. As he once exclaimed, on being assailed relentlessly in a debate on measures originally introduced when the then Opposition was in office: "They are your children! Can't you recognise them because they happen to be in my arms?"

In the end, disgusted with politics, Tardieu left Parliament and devoted himself to pitiless dissection of the regime in a series of books which sickness did not prevent him to finish. His analysis of the crying evil of the Third Republic – "politics as a profession" - was as masterly as it was accurate. But he could not escape the reproach that he himself had accepted the situation for many years, had benefited by it, and had never even attempted to remedy it when in power. His opponents ascribed much of his bitterness to wounded pride, and his relative failure in politics to his sense of superiority and reluctance to compromise.

The tragedy of André Tardieu's career was that, when the crisis came, he should be stricken by a disease which left him a wreck physically and mentally. He had looked upon life as a fight – and loved it as such. In all he had attempted he had come out on top. Suddenly he was snuffed out. Had health continued, one may wonder whether Philippe Pétain might not have called upon him instead of Pierre Laval in June 1940. Certainly a fighter was needed then.

Laval, the team-mate, was the reverse. Compromise, trades, deals are his very lifeblood. Canny son of canny Auvergne, he is a peasant through and through. A democrat? Scarcely, though he has methodically made it appear that he is close to the people. An aristocrat? Scarcely, though he owns a château and his daughter married a dapper count. A statesman? Scarcely, because he lacks breadth of view. A politician? Most assuredly, because he is a born trader. Had he remained in his native village he would have traded horses or cattle; because he entered Parliament he learned how to trade votes and rapidly became expert.

Pierre Laval, of course, was not to be seen in the circles frequented by Bennett. He was uncouth and still is – indelicate also, if measured by the standards of Madame Darblay who labelled all the French so "because they will spit upon any place". Laval's chauffeur is witness to that: "He is not a bad boss, but I do wish he wouldn't use the car as a cuspidor". These were not manners for La Lanterne, Bennett's hunting lodge at Versailles, built by Louis XV for one of his favourites. Moreover, Laval's electors, "horny-handed sons of toil", would not have understood.

I met Laval for the first time many years later, having trouble with his plate of peas in a fashionable restaurant. He comes into the picture at this stage because of the "tandem". In those days he was slowly making his way – and his money – both as lawyer and as politician; learning how to be a good mixer, shaking hands, passing wisecracks, laughing at other people's jokes, exchanging confidences in secluded corners – every trick of the trade. Naturally he prospered. At first his opinions were decidedly Left; in the normal course of things they veered to Moderate. In time he became Parliament's champion manipulator of votes. When Tardieu failed to convince by force of logical exposition, Laval won the battle by individual encounters in the lobbies, swaying waverers not so much by reason or by sentiment as by interest.

Small wonder then that when Marshal Pétain needed a man to induce Parliament to abdicate on July 11, 1940, his choice fell on Pierre Laval. It was good work, cleverly done. And the setting, the theatre at Vichy, gave ironical emphasis to the histrionics. For several days, whether in private or public session of Senate or of Chamber, Laval exerted his talents to the full, wheedling here, cajoling there, instilling everywhere a spirit of compromise. His triumph came when the two Houses, sitting as the National Assembly, virtually voted themselves out of existence. Considered in retrospect, that day marked the summit of Laval's career. With infinite cunning he invoked Pétain's name for his every act, his every promise, culminating with: "For France I thank you in the Marshal's name." Small wonder again, therefore, that when Pétain needed someone to negotiate with the German occupant the choice fell on Pierre Laval, the man whose name remains the same whichever way you look at it.

It may be that at that time Laval was genuinely animated by patriotic motives – or convinced himself that he was. It may be that, infatuated with self-confidence, he believed sincerely that he could worst the Germans in that finassieren which Gustav Stresemann had practised so successfully on Aristide Briand. It may be … Furthermore, all this may be pleaded in extenuation when the day of judgment comes; it may even be advanced then that, despite all appearances, Laval really was working for the United Nations. If he senses the possibility of supping with the Devil, of a surety his long spoon will be ready. Yet the American correspondents who faced him

146

in Vichy towards the end of that fateful July cannot but doubt. For five minutes on that occasion Pierre Laval raised the mask. The face behind was not pretty, but it was revealing.

Had his wife been by his side, the mask might have remained unraised. Her husband's ascent has not blunted Madame Laval's innate common sense. When news photographers made pictures at Chateldon, the family estate, it was she who suggested that it might be well to remove the bust of Benito Mussolini adorning the study. It was she also who, when they left, said very practically: "In any case your photographs will be good publicity for our mineral water". For Chateldon lies in the region of medicinal springs which made Vichy famous before it became merely notorious. And Pierre Laval is not above making an honest penny on the side. His mineral water if labelled "Sergental" – pinchbeck Vichy bottled by a pinchbeck Talleyrand.

But Madame Laval was not there that day. The atmosphere was not congenial, for there was a pretence that the correspondents had sought the audience, which was not the fact. But Laval soon recovered his poise. In the centre of a room in his suite at the Hôtel du Parc, he sat at a small round table, swarthy, blotchy, ugly, arms sprawled, a fag-end in one corner of a mouth itching to expectorate. There came instant recollection of urchin days and of catching toads "to make them smoke".

This toad not only puffed at his cigarette, but it spoke – with venom. Punctuating phrases with characteristic grunts – "Hein!" – Laval fustigated "all those people who have done France so much harm – the Jews, the Socialists, the Communists, the British Empire". When a confrère ventured the suggestion that British victory was the only hope of recovering Alsace and Lorraine he lost all measure. He foamed as he lashed England and the English; it was literally painful to hear. Then, in conclusion: "The English got me in 1935; they won't get me again". The allusion was to his fall from office, caused by the anticipatory revelation of his agreement with Sir Samuel Hoare to placate Italy at the time of her Ethiopian venture.

When the correspondents compared impressions after the audience there was unanimity. From his own mouth Pierre Laval stood on record. He sided with Germany because of his personal grudge against England and he would rather lose Alsace and Lorraine than see them restored by success of British arms. Thus was revealed an unsuspected aspect of "collaboration" with Germany. Laval had said also: "The English are doomed. By October all will be over." This, mind you, was in July 1940.

So sure was he that the war was nearing its end that despite his canniness he cast discretion to the winds and "went German" so earnestly that Pétain rebelled on discovering what was obvious – he was serving as cloak. Moreover Laval had brought with him – and installed in lucrative posts – a wondrous retinue, surpassing even Falstaff's in rag, tag, and bobtail. From paunchy confidential secretary to lean and hungry hangers-on, mostly on the fringe of journalism, these men flaunted their easily-won titles, smirked, postured, cavorted, intrigued, vying one with the other in insolence, arrogance and meanness. Their girl friends were there, too, even more brazen. Laval was paying old debts from the public purse – and a swarm of locusts descended upon Vichy. In all fairness it must be said that when François Darlan, Admiral of the Fleet, succeeded him there came another swarm, equally ravenous but of another hue – navy-blue.

Marshal Pétain had his own following, just as ambitious and avid for power, but better dressed, better mannered, more discreet, almost gentlemanly and – redeeming feature! –

opposed to "collaboration". The twain could never meet, the more so since the aforesaid chauffeur – he made much money carrying clandestine correspondence to Paris under his master's very nose – told all and sundry: "Just you wait until we get rid of that old fogey and see what we'll do!"

So it came to pass that on December 13, 1940, a Friday, Pierre Laval was deprived of all his office and shorn of all his glory. 'Twas near the witching hour. Because Pétain dined late and retired late, much midnight oil was burned in Vichy. Laval had come to the Hôtel du Parc some hours earlier, as confident as ever. He left a virtual prisoner. The scene was dramatic. By eleven o'clock some three score had learned that something was toward, the trunks and boxes bearing Pétain's name were being collected as if for a journey – and with ostentation. Did this portend abdication or revolution? Soon the word passed that Laval had fallen from grace. This time at any rate, he could not accuse the English!

The throng was hushed, all eyes turned to the wide staircase. Few minutes later, Laval appeared, preceded and followed by police officers. Outside it was bitterly cold. His head was sunk in the fur collar of his coat, his hat was crushed to his eyes; his right arm pressed a brief-case. He scowled as he was whisked through the revolving door. It was a vengeful scowl. Within forty-eight hours his German friends were in Vichy and a giant in feldgrau, gun at the ready, stood guard over the apartment of His Excellency Otto Abetz, Ambassador of the Reich. Abetz and Laval left for Paris together. The sequel is history. Some sixteen months later, thanks to the same friends, Pierre Laval returned to office – and his swarm with him. His power was greater but his confidence less, for in the interval a French youth who did not like "collaboration" had pumped bullets into his carcass.

149

But this book is not a history of France and the fourth of these Premiers, Paul Reynaud, needs to be introduced. Before parting with Laval, however, it should be said that he failed utterly to comprehend America. In 1930 he had gone to Washington and had been received by Herbert Hoover at the White House. But the trip had taught him little. He assumed to the last, for instance, that the American press was as the French, to be bought with decorations, dinners or mere pelf. Had he not his own "American mouthpiece" in the person of the correspondent of a news service who had accompanied him on that journey? And had he not the good fortune of being able to feel the American pulse through his son-in-law Count René de Chambrun, who enjoyed citizenship as a direct descendant of La Fayette and spoke glibly of what "I told Roosevelt"? Because of these influences, Pierre Laval, even today, has not realised that he stinks in American nostrils. So with his henchmen. They would slink to the American Embassy in Vichy to tell the attachés there how in reality, like their chief, they loved America. Whereat Admiral William D. Leahy would smile his dryest.

Now for Paul Reynaud. It was because of Bennett that I first saw and heard him. The story is worth telling in detail.

More than once in my presence the Commodore would instruct a servant to call the cashier at the business office. After a few seconds the telephone bell would ring. "Is that you? I want some money. Take a taxi, at my expense, and bring me 10, 000 francs." The cashier would come and produce a wad of bills which Bennett would crumple into a vest pocket. And he would depart – without asking for a receipt. Bennett would have gasped had he requested any acknowledgement of the sum; instant dismissal probably would have been his lot. The Commodore never could have understood why he should give a receipt for his own money. "Book-keeping by single entry was good enough for my father and it's good enough for me", he would say, for he had absolutely no concept of accounts. In his eyes money for the *Herald* and money for his own use came from the same source – the cashier. And that was all there was to it.

It took years to induce him to agree to an annual audit of the books by a firm of certified accountants, but no power on earth could have prevailed upon him to permit those accountants to inquire into his personal affairs. Which explains why, just before the First World War, his own cashier decamped with 200 000 francs ($40 000 gold dollars).

One Sunday morning – when Bennett was in Paris we worked Sundays – he telephoned me to come at once. He did not ask: "Is that you?" or mention a taxi "at my expense", so that I gathered something out of the ordinary had happened. With livid face he handed me a letter. It was a confession from the man, begging for mercy – and promising to repay in instalments. My immediate reaction was: "It can't be *Herald* money, Mr Bennett; it must be from your private account." That hit him between wind and water. Although it all came from the same purse, he might have looked upon the loss of *Herald* money almost with equanimity, as one of those accidents which must occur in business. But to steal from his private account was a crime indeed, in which insult was added to injury. It was lèse-majesté, high treason, heinous to a degree.

Nor did it improve matters when I explained how, because he would not tolerate any auditing of his private account and would give no receipts, it was the easiest thing in the world to bring him 10 000 francs and debit him 20 000. I rubbed it in because I felt revengeful that day. This cashier had been recommended by "ladies running a charity in the form of an employment agency". One morning Bennett had told me all about this sort of philanthropy: "I met Countess Blank on the avenue yesterday and she explained her organisation. You can

151

find everything you need there" – (here a leer at me) – "even a managing editor. And they are all highly recommended. I've just taken a cashier from them, a very good man who was once in the Chinese Customs Service which still owes him a lot of money." That Sunday consequently when Bennett wound up by asking: "What's to be done?" I answered bluntly: "Put the police on his track, if only as a duty to society. The man is dangerous and should be stopped."

Bennett hesitated. He did not relish the attendant publicity. Finally he acquiesced and I drove post haste to police headquarters. How he must have regretted that assent! Next day the papers were full of the story, which really was good. It was discovered that the man had a room in a small hotel, but merely as an accommodation address. He had taken a villa in a pleasant suburb where he led a gay life with several mistresses. He was traced from Paris to Marseille, from Marseille to Algiers, from Algiers to London, there to be arrested and extradited. The chase had lasted a month during which newspaper interest had not flagged. Then came the trial – with more publicity. The attorney for the defence took the easy line of abusing the other side: "That fabulously wealthy American who paid a miserable wage to a poor man and placed in his way almost irresistible temptation." His client got three years, but with suspended sentence. The court added rather platonically that he should refund the money.

Five years later I saw the fellow again – for ten seconds. It was the very day I was demobilised. With a brother officer we were celebrating the occasion with lunch in a good restaurant. From our table we could see every one coming down from the first floor. We were sipping coffee when down the stairs appeared a flashy woman followed by a prosperous looking man – Bennett's former cashier. Catching my eye, he stopped dead. Then drawing his companion back, he retraced his steps and disappeared. Another five years later a begging letter reached me, addressed: "The Director, *Paris Times*". Therein the signatory explained that he had been "in the Chinese Customs Service, which still owes me a lot of money." I replied: "You will remember my name. Shall I send your letter to the police?"

I sat in court when the cashier was tried. The name of his attorney was Paul Reynaud, a dapper little man, very self-possessed and very self-asserting, who, one felt, would certainly make his way. I, for one, had never heard of him before. Had Walt Disney characters existed then, Reynaud would have been dubbed "Mickey Mouse". The sobriquet fits him to a nicety and no further description is necessary. He had more than one string to his bow, practised law, dabbled in politics and familiarised himself with business. He served very honourably during the First World War and returned more than ever determined to make his mark. Astute developments of interests in Mexico City assured material independence and enabled him to devote more time to politics. Never daunted by obstacles, he won some very hard fought elections; once in the Chamber of deputies he soon came to the fore as debater. Cabinet rank followed in due course and it became manifest that he had set his mind on becoming Prime Minister someday. Yet he had to wait long, probably because of "Mickey Mouse".

Meantime he spoke with versatility on all subjects, particularly financial and economic, and he let it be understood that he had his own remedies for many of the ills that beset the world. For a time he sat among the Moderates, with Tardieu and Laval, but he was ever prepared to trim his sails if that were calculated to facilitate the attainment of his ambitions. Loyalty to a chief was scarcely his strong point. He knew the value of publicity and never disdained it. The public came to know him through photographs – in a pith helmet as Minister of Colonies, riding a bicycle or swimming in a pool as an advocate of physical exercise. Yet he was fated to wait until the Second

World War had entered its critical phase before he was called upon to head a Cabinet.

The very day on which he faced the Chamber of Deputies he obtained its confidence by a margin of one single vote. "Mickey" as ever, he refused to resign and bluffed his way through by defying Parliament to swap horses while crossing a stream – the campaign in Norway was then turning adversely for the Allies. He was fated also to be a constant bearer of ill tidings. Things had come to such a point that the mere announcement of a broadcast by Paul Reynaud made men wonder what fresh disaster had befallen. Then his rasping voice would come over the air with studied delivery – one was prepared to learn that the words had been rehearsed again and again, with each phrase, each paragraph duly timed.

In form as in substance these broadcasts were the speeches of a renowned trial lawyer seeking to befuddle the jury and browbeat the bench. With tremulous voice he would strike the pathetic chord, then in heroic mood announce what he was determined to do, ringing the changes on "energy" and "confident resolution" and "new methods with new men". It was he who proclaimed that "we have cut Germany's road to Scandinavian ore", and it was he who branded the King of the Belgians as a "felon". He even broadcast in English – of a sort. But it all sounded hollow to men of discernment.

Last came, in June 1940 that tragic, pathetic, heart-rending appeal to the United States to enter the war forthwith that democracy might be saved. Already the Germans had overrun half the country. The French armies were cut up. Ten million folk were fleeing ever further south. The government itself was on the run, still broadcasting brave words but leading the way. What could Washington do, at a distance of 3,000 miles? No man in his senses could believe that the appeal was based on reason; it was sheer hysterics. And so it was accepted by most. They realised that it was the death-knell.

Yet Paul Reynaud is no fool, far from it. Is it possible that he was sincere that day, that it was not just one more speech? Did he really believe that Franklin D. Roosevelt, at his behest, would ask Congress to plunge into war a country that was not ready? It seems inconceivable. More than once I heard the remark: "Oui, mais c'est loin l'Amérique!" ("Yes, but America is far off!").

The fact is that for too many years in French political circles words not only had come to lose their meaning, but oratory had come to be considered an end in itself. All emphasis was on speech; it had replaced action. "Energetic discourse by the Prime Minister", newspapers would say in their headlines. Paul Reynaud in particular suffered from that complex. To prove his foresight and to demonstrate his statesmanship, he set great store on speeches made five or six years previously, so much so that in wartime he published a volume in which they were reprinted. None could gainsay that he had advocated the creation of armoured divisions, that he had urged the necessity of a professional army and even outlined its composition, that he had proposed the construction of so many tanks and so many airplanes. In which connection he invoked the technical authority of General Charles de Gaulle, thus enabling him, should occasion arise, to claim affinity with the Free French.

But Reynaud could not show that, once in power, he had striven to pass from words to acts; never had he made more tanks and more airplanes a condition of accepting office; never had he threatened to resign if the system he proposed was rejected. So with his subsequent open letters to Marshal Pétain; they serve to place him on record, but nothing more. History is likely to write him down as a clever lawyer, and that is all.

155

Politically, was he a democrat? Frankly, no. Was he a demagogue? Perhaps not. Rather he was the product of that perversion of the parliamentary system which brought disaster to France. Purely artificial and always opportunist, it ignored realities and set store only on lobby intrigues, developing a morbid lust for patronage and power – power not only to further political causes but to serve personal ends. While war was being waged, Reynaud's great concern was to modify the divorce law so that he might marry his mistress!

These three Premiers – in reality four, like the Three Musketeers – had all been to America and had all failed to understand America. The reason may be discovered perhaps in the fact that they based their appraisal mostly on the expatriates they had met.

CHAPTER 10

FAR FROM HOME

To discuss expatriates is a delicate matter, even for a native American. It is so easy to become biased. Moreover, what is an expatriate? And after how many years abroad does the designation apply? In fairness, each case should be considered on its merits. Yet expatriates have played so important a part in forming European opinion of America that they cannot be ignored, especially in France, always a favoured place of residence. Remember that the American colony in Paris officially came into existence at a Fourth of July dinner which Thomas Jefferson gave in 1789. There grew about these early comers a legend which persisted long, that of the rich and eccentric American.

In the days of the "Directoire" relations with America had become strained; periodic attacks were made on American ships and the French Government even went so far as to refuse to receive Charles Cotesworth Pinckney, sent as Minister plenipotentiary. There was no marked improvement under Napoleon, but with the end of his empire Paris became a great centre for the counting-houses of American merchant princes. The days of clipper ships saw this phase at its apogee. Quite a number of the settlers were of Puritan stock and much of their activity turned to prayer meetings and religious work of many kinds. There was, for instance, Samson Vryling Stoddard, from Massachusetts, who founded several Bible societies in France. Some of these merchant princes never returned home; their children married into French families.

The general verdict then was that Americans were a strange people, which opinion has scarcely changed since. The next phase confirmed that view. The expatriate of this period ending with the revolution of 1848 is well typified by Colonel Thorn. Research has failed to reveal his origin, even his given name, but, beginning in 1835, the innumerable Parisian weekly sheets devoted to tittle-tattle were filled with his doings – his parties, his receptions, his munificence. He was described variously as "a financial potentate" or "the American colossus". Princesse de Béthune and Duchesse de Rohan were his social sponsors who overlooked his lists of guests. Manifestly very wealthy, he spent lavishly. He leased a historic mansion, furnished it sumptuously; his domestics numbered twenty-five, all in resplendent liveries. There is record of a costume ball he gave in 1840 which took Paris by storm. Thenceforward he was dubbed "an American who can become thoroughly French in taste".

The rising of 1848 extinguished both Louis-Philippe and Colonel Thorn. But, during the reign of Napoleon III a number of Americans again figured in society and court circles. There was, for instance, Lillie Greenough, of Boston, who came to Paris to study music, married Charles Moulton and left a sheaf of piquant letters. There was also Dr Thomas W. Evans, who arrived in 1847 at the age of twenty-three, became partner with Cyrus S. Brewster in the rue de la Paix, "dentists to Their Majesties", and facilitated Empress Eugénie's escape when the crash came in 1870.

Already in those days a change was coming in the composition of the American colony, with a vanguard of business men and students, mostly of art, until under the Third Republic expatriates became divided into three classes.

There was first the expatriate by necessity, the American man or woman whose occupation demanded a period of foreign service. In my experience at least, most of them remained American to the core. They sent their children to American schools, supported American institutions and frequented other Americans. They accepted certain native ways, which was inevitable, but they adapted them to American ways rather than the reverse. In the case of the expatriate by necessity, absence made the heart grow fonder.

There was also the part-time expatriate, himself divided into three categories. The one because he was interested in art or archaeology or languages, or occupied in research; students could be grouped in this class. The other because he was cutting expenses. The third in order to enjoy by entertaining, social consideration possibly lacking at home. It pleased some to be addressed obsequiously in the third person: "Would Madame like this?" or "What are Monsieur's wishes for dinner?" One man I knew was a part-time expatriate for the purpose of establishing his divorcee wife in European society, so that, by repercussion, she might be received in the best circles at home. It grieved him to spend so much money, but it was unavoidable since the general run of newspapers in Europe did not print "society news" for nothing. By great persistency and the least possible outlay he attained his end.

The third variety was the expatriate by choice. He tended to "go native". In France he might become more French than the French, in England more English than the English; he was ever more royalist than the king. On occasion he would not hesitate to declare his country in the wrong. But in time of stress he would remember that he was a citizen of the United States and claim the protection of Uncle Sam. He loved the cheap flattery of the narrow circle in which he moved; above all he loved titles and medals.

There were other varieties and sub-varieties, most of which also came within my purview. There was the much-

159

divorced woman, still young, who finally married a prince of royal house virtually in his dotage. Since the house refused to recognise the union, her single purpose in life was to induce the *Herald* to print the initials "S.A.R." (Her Royal Highness) before her name. There was a papal baron who entertained lavishly and pestered us to publish the names of his guests, all foreign. There was a former member of the House of Representatives who insisted that mention of his parties should appear only in the French section of the paper. There were also shyster lawyers, including one notorious maker of affidavits.

The impression of America produced by this motley crowd was rather confused. Certainly it would have been false had it not been counterbalanced by exploration of student circles. For instance, there existed then in Paris an American Art Association which was American indeed and where could be discerned a trend of deep interest because it pointed to the advent of a truly American school of painting. Its members were earnest seekers. Before their time the practice had been too general not only to study under leading French artists, but also, consciously or unconsciously, to accept their standards and sedulously to imitate them. At the annual Salons, only reference to the catalogue revealed that American works were to be found on the walls. At the Art Association's shows, on the other hand, there was a feeling of something different, a striving not so much after the new or the extreme as was the case after the First World War, but to break with European traditions and to evolve American forms, unshackled. Now, some thirty years later, this has been achieved – American artists have come into their own. Modern American art and modern American literature, to my mind, are more characteristic of America than any other phase of national life – Grant Wood with his "American Gothic", Arnold Friedman with his "Unemployable", and the "Ash-can School".

In those days Montparnasse was peopled – sparsely at that – by painters who actually painted and writers who actually wrote. And Montparnasse was still rustic. There were dairy farms in the Rue Campagne Première, while in the Rue Léopold-Robert hens scuttled off as one passed. The Dôme was a modest café; there were no night clubs and dissipation was of the unsophisticated kind. Montparnasse was merely an offshoot of the classic Latin Quarter.

The writers who had settled there were seekers also. The generation was passing which not only accepted French influence but even wrote in French – Stuart Merrill, Francis Viélé Griffin, Natalie Clifford Barney. Among the newcomers some merely sought the opportunity to write leisurely in congenial and inexpensive surroundings. Others, like the painters, were bent on experiment. Gertrude Stein's salon was not without influence on both. Some speak of a "Paris School of American Literature". It may be a convenient means of classification but it is highly probable that the revolutionaries and the innovators would have revolutionised and innovated equally well at home.

One also met American tourists. But before the First World War their number was relatively small. Moreover, travel still being costly, they did not truly present a cross-section of the United States.

From all these classes the average American appeared thus in the first decade of the century, defined, as if fit, in the vernacular: gregarious, a joiner and good mixer. Intense, active, full of vitality and pep, yet in certain aspects hesitant, not physically but intellectually, as exemplified in a marked desire for consultation. Great capacity for enthusiasm – a quality which carries its own faults. More impulsive than reasoning. Very matter-of-fact, yet readily focussing on abstractions. Intent on learning things; therefore a great questioner, with a tendency to accept as truth whatever he may be told. Clever yet often a sucker. Endowed with a measure of disarming puerility. Of curious and alert mind, ever ready to venture and to experiment. Affable, hospitable, charitable. To some extent a proselytising visionary. In fine, charming yet bewildering.

Inevitably, this appraisal was based in no small degree on contrasts with the average Frenchman. The outstanding difference seemed to be that the latter remained persistently analytical. He reviewed the probable consequences of his every move and, having done so, hesitated to act, where the American would apply the hit-or-miss method and, on the material plane, end up either millionaire or pauper. That contrast is still paramount in its influence on relations between France and the United States. The concepts are so far apart that it is a problem to conciliate them. In its essence the difference is between an old country and a new. Equality of opportunity is the American gospel; equality of possession might be the French. One makes for levelling up, the other for levelling down.

Here again may be traced the influence of the French Revolution. Among rights then won was the right to possess. It has been guarded jealously since. Your true Frenchman yearns to own something, land for preference, for generally he is of peasant stock – something tangible to which he can cling to in the event of new upheavals. He does not yearn for very much because small possessions are easier to preserve and because he is modest in his needs. So that the general ambition is to become a "small proprietor". Everything conspires to make the average Frenchman "small" – his tastes, his inheritance laws, his innate thrift. Therefore "petit" is the typical French qualitative. The mass of the population consists of small landholders, small artisans, small merchants, who aspire to become small investors or small pensioners, living with a small family in a small house with a small garden. Moreover France is the land of small salaries, even for the highest positions. The danger is that "small" may easily degenerate into "petty".

All this smallness has its effect on international intercourse. It makes for insistence on the letter of the bond rather than on its spirit, on immediate minor advantages rather than eventual major ones. Universal in thought and words, the French tend to be parochial in action. Hence they are never quite at ease in international conferences; they will describe in eloquent periods the abstract object to be reached but will haggle over each concrete proposition. They are as charming and bewildering to Americans as Americans are charming and bewildering to them. They understand perfectly – until the moment for getting down to business. In the period before the First World War all this was of no great consequence. Unfortunately the war – and the peace that followed – did not bring greater understanding of national characters and temperaments, although it did produce many lasting individual friendships. So far as I was concerned it advanced my quest considerably.

So a legend grew that Americans were a nation of wealthy eccentrics. They gave it substance by their liberality – due in part to lack of knowledge of local habits – and their readiness to answer appeals to the purse. This instilled the idea that the arrival anywhere of any American was an occasion for largesse – with regrettable moral effect. It induced the French to hold out a hand, first among the lowly, then by a normal process among those who should not have stooped to beg. There is no impugning the sincerity of American philanthropy, of which there have been so many examples in France. Yet some of the more thoughtful could not repress a sense of humiliation that it should be foreign gold which restored such national treasures as Rheims Cathedral or Versailles Palace.

163

Money brings misunderstandings between individuals, even between kin. So it is between nations. From the first it has periodically clouded Franco-American relations – the American Revolutionary debt to France, the long drawn-out Claims question, the French war debt to America. In most cases difficulties arose from the French weakness for mixing sentiment with business. Yet the number of such differences and the fact that generally they ended in agreement, if only tacit, go to prove the existence of fundamental forces making for understanding between the two nations. So may it be when peace returns to this sorely-tried world! For war should change complacent conceptions of values. I have seen two – actor in the first, spectator in the second. Are my sons to see another?

CHAPTER 11

BLOOD AND MIRE

War in any case overshadows all else in a man's life. But how to describe it? As a historian? Possibly, but that would call for many volumes and still be imperfect; too many documents long remain unavailable. As a participant, a witness? Yes, but only as in an early cinematograph film, blurred and jerky. Let me present one reel.

It unwinds in August 1914 with millions of men scanning their Army books. The cover opens on a coloured card marked: "Mobilisation Order". It tells when and where to join – first day, second day, other days. Entrain at Place Hébert or some such unknown place. In time of peace no Parisian ever heard of Place Hébert. There is a freight-yard there, familiar only to car-men. But with war that freight-yard becomes important.

In groups of two score, men pile into box-cars, infantry reservists who have left home and families to kill and be killed. Some shout: "On to Berlin!" Some are full of wine, and sing. But most are silent, struck dumb by events beyond their understanding, above all beyond their control. Already they feel that they are no longer men, but numbers.

The long train puffs out slowly. It stops often – there are so many other trains before it. They come from all points, but there is only one destination – eastward, the front. Everybody says: "The Front", but without any idea of what it means. As the train passes, old men gaze at it wistfully. Women and girls wave their hands or cast flowers – as at a funeral. At wayside stations stand white-haired groups in Sunday black, medals on their breasts. They fought in 1870, two generations before. Now they are saluting sons and grandsons on the same errand. At one town a bishop leads them, right hand raised in blessing.

The August sun beats on the cars. Men doff coats. Some lie on the filthy floor to sleep. Others eat and drink. With old-soldier wisdom they explain: "Break a crust when you may. You never know when the next will come". Others talk without cease, mostly to tell of what they have left behind. Such talk may not be cheerful, yet it proves comforting. Dwelling on the past, it serves to veil the future.

Individuals are fast welding into an anonymous mass, whose acts henceforth will be responses to commands – mass reflexes, mass thoughts even. As the train crawls through a station an officer runs alongside shouting: "The Germans have poisoned lots of canned food. Pass the word along." No one questioned his announcement. Docilely some bring out pencil stubs and scribble to wives: "Beware of all canned foods. Some are poisoned." They have not the least idea whether they will be able to mail these notes.

The train chugs and stops, chugs and stops. Night falls. Men ask drowsily: "Where are we? Where are we going?" No one answers because no one knows. And to tell the truth probably no one cares. Fate is at the helm and nothing can alter Fate. Near the track a call rings out: "Halt! What goes there?" It rouses the sleepers, awed by this reminder of war, with steel striking steel as a breech-lock opens. Another voice calls: "France!" The dialogue proceeds: "Advance France and give the countersign!" Merely a sentry on the line challenging the rounds. But it brings silence to the train.

At last the locomotive ceases its chugging, seemingly for good. It is past midnight – ten hours to travel little more than one hundred miles. There is a guard in this large station and light from gas-jets play on bayonets as officers order the men out. In the dark they stumble through deserted streets to infantry barracks where they give their names and are sorted into squads, platoons, companies. They stumble upstairs, then stumble down again, for already the whole place is filled with sleepers – snoring, grunting, hiccoughing, and frowzy.

Others are directed to more distant places of assembly. I am of the number. We go to cavalry barracks vacated by squadrons days ago. In the guardroom a sergeant with a long-service badge scarcely deigns to look at us. He is too busy talking to a friend just arrived. One hears such phrases as: "Where's Jack? Oh, he's gone to the war!" So, one reflects, the war is not here. Where is it? And what is it? And why do some go to the war and some remain here. This place too, is crowded with sleeping men. Finally we drift into the riding-school, there to lie on the tan. But we cannot sleep; the huge shed is drafty and nights in August may be cold.

Dawn finds us shivering. We shake out the tan and roam about the barracks. I discover my company. The captain remembers me. "Mighty glad to see you", he says, "for God knows there's work to do". And for forty-eight hours there is no rest. Mobilisation instructions are minute; every ten minutes something has to be fetched from somewhere – equipment, arms, munitions, rations. Yet it all seems utterly chaotic. When a man walks into the company office and introduces himself as a sergeant or corporal, you want to hug him – at least somebody with responsibility and authority! You cram him into a uniform – and pin on his stripes.

Every hour or so there is an attempt at roll-call. Soon one knows the names by heart. The problem is to find the

167

individuals answering to them. Some of those names are strange. "Taillefumier" (Dungcutter) for instance. There should be two of them – brothers. But they fail to reply. "Taillefumier! Taillefumier!" The others laugh, pinch their nostrils, make coarse jokes.

Nerves become frayed. Men walk in and out of the office. All ask for something – coats or packs, food or drink. They leave when told to go to hell. A Dominican monk appears in white robe and sandals. "Oh go to hell! No, pardon me. You're looking for B Company? Further along the corridor." A lieutenant fusses around. He wants an orderly and he can't open his field-chest. He asks for a knife to force the lock. I hand him mine. He smashes a blade and fusses the more. "Oh, go to … I mean let me have a try." Another blade snaps. There is a general feeling that we are going to have trouble with this lieutenant. But we can't help it. Everything is in the hands of Fate. Soon Fate transfers him to a machine-gun section and a German bullet drills a hole in his head.

More roll-calls. "Taillefumier! Taillefumier!" It seems hopeless. But suddenly the brothers answer. Others too. That marks the turning point. Order comes out of chaos and when the colonel rides into the barrack square to present the colours, the regiment has taken shape. Drums roll, bugles blare. Manifestly the Old Man is deeply moved. He voices his satisfaction, speaks of abstractions – Honour, Duty, Discipline. In conclusion there is something concrete – we entrain at dusk.

This relieves the tension. In the company we eat sausages reeking of garlic, wash it down with wine. Even the fussy lieutenant unbends, regrets my broken knife, sends for more drink. His man returns with news that there is a strong guard at the gate. Having at last gathered his flock, the colonel is taking no chances. Fourteen hours later the regiment detrains at Verdun.

The film rolls on, as blurred as ever. No one knows what is happening. No mail, no newspapers. The one thing certain is that the war is still on. Guns boom in the distance. They must be German, for we have only "75's" – and they bark. Farm wagons lumber along filled with wounded men, ashen pale, biting their lips that they may not cry with pain. A battalion comes from the firing-line; a tall private stands out, red-haired, bareheaded, marching as if in sleep, eyes in vacant stare. He sees none of the things about him; he is living yesterday over again.

Now the regiment is in position. We gather that we belong to the "fixed defence of Verdun". Beyond that we know nothing. But there is a feeling abroad that all is not going well. We learn that men have charged gallantly but have been mowed down by machine-guns unexpectedly numerous. Field regulations instructed that the enemy must be attacked wherever seen. He was. But the feldgrau seem numberless. Each morning the observation balloons ringing Verdun rise nearer the city than they did the day before. That does not augur well. Finally they rise no more.

Miles to the south-east tongues of flame spit from what might be a phantasmal battleship on a sea of clouds; the enemy is attacking a fort. The menace draws nearer. The Germans are crossing the Meuse. With field-glasses you can sweep a stretch of road down from Montfaucon. It is black with battalions, squadrons, batteries – a stream of men flowing endlessly for two days and two nights. The Crown Prince's army is pushing nach Paris. So sure is he of victory that he does not deign take Verdun on the way. Later he will try for months – and fail. It will cost more than a million lives. Later also there will be an American cemetery at Montfaucon.

From a knoll you can see stirring scenes. Batteries gallop up, unlimber, open fire. Soon they themselves are shelled. Eventually they disappear, going south-west, the direction masses of infantry have been taking in recent days. A hussar regiment wheels into view. It splits into squadrons which deploy and vanish from sight – towards the enemy. Soon they reappear – only to ride away – to the south-west of course. Now groups of uhlans dot the hills. The French armies are in retreat. We remain where we are.

Several days pass and still no one knows anything. Then suddenly we are told that a great battle has been fought and won. In history it is called the Battle of the Marne. The Crown Prince's army appears again on that same stretch of road, but this time going up the hill, not down. Then the Germans halt and dig trenches. So do we.

Our regiment has a new mission. A general order tells us that we have been transformed from fixed into mobile defence. We realise that winning a battle does not end a war. But we welcome the change, because we see new country, make new acquaintances. A lieutenant-colonel accosts us: My name is Lebrun, of the 5th Fortress Artillery. Where can I find your colonel?" He seems a decent sort, not over-assertive. You offer to guide him. He accepts with diffident courtesy. Years later you can say: "The first time I met President Albert Lebrun was in the winter of 1914".

This is as it should be in a democracy – the whole nation in arms, sharing the same hardships, facing the same perils. Yet certain inequalities offend. You hear men from another outfit speaking well of their lieutenant; his name is Loubet, son of a former President of the Republic. But you hear also of X, and Y and Z, politicians or journalists who have blossomed into aides-de-camp. They rush to open the door when their general goes forth in his automobile. And they laugh loud at his jokes.

By now trenches have become continuous. Man has fallen to the level of the beast and yearns for nothing more than food and sleep. We are preparing for a long war and we learn many things. One is that war is inseparable from vermin – rats, mice, fleas, lice. We become filthy for several reasons. One is that we have no possibility of keeping clean. Another is that the soldier soon becomes a fatalist. Why trouble about anything when you know not what the morrow may bring? You may be dead or change sector. The word kokken-modding comes to mind, recalling casual study of prehistory. "Kitchen-midden" is pregnant with meaning now. In billets, dug-outs everywhere, the strata of beef bones, old socks, rotting equipment, garbage of all kinds, reveal the identity of preceding units.

Rats are beginning to abound, even in the woods where we are posted. We live in rudimentary dug-outs, a cross between a trench and a log-cabin. At some distance there is a château, already much battered by shelling. Our predecessors must have visited it, gleaning objects strangely out of keeping with these surroundings – Louis XV clocks and fine china bearing a crest beneath a count's coronet. The countess never dreamed of the use to which we put her best bed-sheets – stretched across the ceiling of our huts to keep the earth heaped overhead from trickling between the logs. Rats have sought lodging even there. The sheet bulges as they pass to and fro. Occasionally a man lies in wait with fixed bayonet. He aims in the centre of the four depressions made by the rat's feet, then thrusts home with full force. A squeak, a clot of blood. But what is one rat less?

Runners bearing orders have become reckless. Rather than scramble through undergrowth they pass along the edge of the wood, marking a regular trail. It must be visible from the observation balloon spying upon us. At intervals the trail is swept with shrapnel. Already three runners have been hit. One died in the dressing station. A private from the Medical Corps brings his belongings. He says: "Please check the estate of the late Paul Durand". The man means well, but one wishes he did not insist so much on Regulations. Estate! An old leather purse with a few francs, a clasp-knife, a pocket-book with some letters and a photograph of a woman and two children. Paul Durand's estate!

From time to time the High Command, that mysterious entity which for us is the embodiment of Fate, sends an order to take a trench, a position, a village. Guns behind us roar for an hour or more. Then over the top; a headlong dash, heart beating fit to burst, temples throbbing from the rush of blood; a blind, mad scamper. If we succeed, the tension cannot relax because there may be a counter-attack. If we fail, there is nothing left but to fall back under a hail of fire.

As night falls wounded men plead pitifully: "Stretcher-bearers! Stretcher-bearers!" Those able to walk creep in. One has his jaw shot away. Nothing can be done for him. He lies there for hours, unuttered groans gurgling through his life-blood. At dawn he dies. The surgeon says: "Why aren't we allowed to put them out of their misery?"

Sometimes the High Command decides that the position must be occupied at whatever cost. Marchéville, for instance, though already several attempts have failed. One day the order passes through the companies: "Send to headquarters at once the names of men who know Marchéville." Several answer. They rub their hands with glee and say: "Sure we're going to be sent to the rear to assist the Staff." A week later they learn that they are assigned as guides to the attacking troops.

Here the film should reproduce two communiqués in facsimile. The first, issued in the spring of 1915, reads: "In an attack on Marchéville our infantry reached the enemy's barbed wire". The second, dated November 10, 1918, the eve of the Armistice, says: "American troops have taken Marchéville".

172

Between those two dates not a word had been said about Marchéville. Our attack had failed. On that barbed wire the dead slowly returned to dust.

The reel switches back to billets. We wonder why they call them rest billets, since we toil more there than in the trenches. Every night, for instance, parties go to the lines, bearing wire, rails, logs. It is hard work, not exempt from danger. Usually the parties are led by the first lieutenant. He grates on our nerves. He will say one night: "Be wary, men! The sky is clear and the moon is full, propitious for an enemy attack." And the next: "Be wary, men! It is pitch dark, propitious for an enemy attack." At heart he is a coward; we know it and he knows that we know it. Soon he is sent to the rear by medical order for "inappetence" – want of inclination. How true! Weeks later we hear that he is in charge of a depot – a blustering bully. Appetence had returned!

The war seems to drag on. To cheer us, no doubt, we are told that enemy morale is low and the blockade so effective that the Germans are short of metal. An order signed: "Joffre" detailing all this is read to us at muster. One passage runs: "It has been noted that the enemy's shells are of poor quality. Many fail to explode." Though we are standing at attention, men nudge each other and smile. From where we stand we can see "big black ones" crashing down not two miles away.

We parade for an inspection by the general commanding our army. He is a tall, handsome man, with remarkable blue eyes. He has the reputation of being a "Republican general". He commends us for what we have done, then asks that a certain sergeant be summoned. That sergeant belongs to my company; his father, a prominent politician, has belonged to several cabinets. Sergeant and general walk up and down the village street for some time, talking. The general

173

leaves. So – after a week – does the sergeant, transferred to a comfortable distance from the lines.

Time drags. War has become a routine. So many days in the trenches, so many days in billets. The monotony is broken by changes of sector or by attacks. You feel more and more a machine. For still you know nothing. Village urchins are better informed. They point to a hill and say: "That's where you'll be at two o'clock tomorrow afternoon." They are right. Officers talk at mess, the batmen hear, they tell the girls, and the girls repeat it at home. Soon everybody knows except those primarily interested. The hill is Les Eparges. Thirty years later, so seared was the soil that grass still refused to grow.

We discard our red pants and caps to don horizon-blue and steel helmets. The enemy begins to use poison-gas and flame-throwers. Short-leave is established; seven days at home every six months. The announcement is welcomed, but some fear that it may betoken a very long war. One description has become popular: "If you leave your hole you're a dead 'un. If Fritz leaves his hole he's a dead 'un. So you and Fritz just stop where you are."

To add to all the other vermin there is red tape. Military bureaucracy appears even worse than the civil variety. As soon as the front becomes established, it runs riot. It comes as a shock, moreover, to discover that the great concern should be for equipment rather than for the men. "Company commanders are reminded that at the end of the campaign they will be responsible for all issues made to their unit and that their responsibility may be pecuniary." The more philosophical shrug their shoulders and say: "It'll be time to talk about that when the campaign does end". Anyhow realisation soon comes that bureaucracy merely wants sheets of paper bearing signatures. Nobody ever dreams of checking what is written.

Shells are falling on the village when a runner dashes into our shelter. He reports that regimental headquarters are calling me urgently by telephone. It is still early in the war and there is only one apparatus in the place. Heads down, wallowing in the mud every time a whiz-bang screeches, the runner and I reach the cellar where the operators are lodged. Panting, I ask: "What's the trouble?"

A clerk-sergeant replies: "Your company records for the last quarters don't tally with the quantities issued you on mobilisation. There's fewer of everything, rifles, equipment, blankets."

"Good God, is that all! It's easy to explain by our casualties."

"No doubt. But the Quarter-master-General can't guess that. Each time anything is lost your captain should make a report. You'll find all about it in the Regulations."

My captain's comment is curt "Damn the Regulations!" Nevertheless we decide to send henceforth periodical reports of losses, real or imaginary, so that our records will always show less than the quantities issued.

The lesson is not lost. At the end of a hard day in pouring rain the company cook appears, indignant, excited: "I can't get the chow warm. All the wood is either green or sodden. And the boys are raising hell. You can hear them from here."

A moment of reflection. Then: "You go to the company wagon. You'll find a lot of tent-pegs put away in bags. We've never set up the tents and we're not likely to. They'll burn fine."

The man hesitates. He must have visions of being shot for "wilful and wanton destruction of Army property".

"Do what you're told. The responsibility is mine." In ten minutes he returns grinning: "Gee, what a blaze! Now the boys are cheering."

That evening the captain signed a report telling how a quantity of tent-pegs had been lost "by action of the enemy". No question was raised. It may not be very ethical, but it is war.

So the reel unfolds, endlessly; week by week, month by month, year by year. More rain, more mud; a terrible winter with its train of frozen limbs; more dirt, more misery. Periodically tragedy enters to break the monotony – offensives, great and small, with attendant slaughter: Champagne, Somme, Chemin des Dames. And Verdun! Horror unspeakable! There seems no limit to the sufferings of poor, tortured flesh.

An epilogue to this first reel:

1. A Victory Parade. Detachments representing Allied and Associated nations march beneath the Triumphal Arch in Paris to the frenzied hurrahs of millions.
2. Everywhere in the battle zone cemeteries are laid out – French, British, American, Italian, Portuguese, Russian, German, Austrian, Bulgarian, Turkish – hundreds of thousands of graves in serried rows.
3. Inscriptions in public transport read: "In this car, seats numbered 1 to 4 are reserved for the maimed and wounded of the war". They were still there in 1939, ready for the next batch

CHAPTER 12

IMPOTENCE OF THE CITIZEN

Such is war – seen through the small end of the telescope. After this reel should come the customary intermission. It will give time to ponder on the fact that in the Europe now passing, war was prepared by diplomats and soldiers but fought by citizens. Mobilisation tore them from hearth and home, clapped them into uniforms, and launched them into the fray. For many the change was too sudden.

On a battle plan there are regiments, divisions, army corps – pawns to be moved on the chessboard. But in reality there are only mortal men, all of a common clay. They may turn into heroes if inspired by an ideal, but even then the process needs time. Certainly many characters are tempered by the ordeal. But what of the mass?

In the First World War, for example, there was the 15th Army Corps, from Marseille. In August 1914 it was a pawn, moved north many miles and hurled against the enemy alongside such crack troops as the 20th Corps, then commanded by Foch – with my old Iron Division. On the map this seems normal – a straight line connects Marseille and Morhange, in Lorraine. Morhange was a tragedy. Against superior forces entrenched in strong positions, well equipped with machine-guns, even the Iron Division lost its dash. The 15th Corps wavered and fell back, with gunners cutting the traces and abandoning their pieces. The transition had been too swift for these Southerners, care-free baskers in the sun. Yet, once inured, they proved as good as the others.

This 15th Corps is recalled, not because of futile controversies long forgotten, but because of personal contact. Its next position adjoined ours. We found these soldiers honest, homely folk, to whom Lorraine was almost a foreign land. All was strange to them, people as well as surroundings. They arrived at night-fall and clapped hands at a familiar sight – vines trailed from prop to prop. It comforted southern hearts. Dawn dispelled the illusion. The vines were barbed wire. Dawn brought also a pitiful sight – stragglers herded by armed guards, with a provost-marshal, red with rage, shouting: "You ought all to be shot! Yes, all shot! Shot as examples! Yes, as examples!" Few months later his shouts still rang in my ears as Clown met his end.

We were at Fresnes-en-Woëvre as Christmas was drawing near. All was wet, muddy, gloomy. On these flats stretching to the east of Verdun, the more you dig the more water you meet. So the trenches were mostly parapet – sand-bags, steel rails, logs, with here and there a mattress. The line was not yet continuous. Through the intervals parties from both sides roamed and often clashed. Reserves were held in the village, frequently on alarm. Fresnes is almost a market-town. A stream runs through its main street. Back from the trenches the only way to rid oneself of mud was to dump everything into the water, coat, boots, and rifle. The trouble was to dry them again. And Fresnes stank abominably. As is the custom in Lorraine, a manure-pile stood before each house. When the Germans sent over large shells, which was often, one at least would plaster the walls with dung.

Our company was assigned the lawyer's house. He must have been prosperous, for it was large, with piano in the parlour and hot-house in the garden. He must have been cultured, too, for the approach to the latrines was strewn with pages torn from the classics in his library.

Not a pane of glass was left in the village; many roofs had caved in, many walls had fallen. Not a man stirred in the street, though some crept round back-gardens to the hardware store or the druggist's to see if per chance there were still some pickings – a box of cough tablets, a knife or a ball of string. All was silent, except when heavy guns in the lawyer's flower-beds opened fire and the enemy replied.

It was cold, but there was plenty of wood, though little time and less inclination to saw it. "What's that noise in the barn next door?" I asked Michel one morning. I was company sergeant-major then and Michel was the handyman; he figured on the roll as liaison cyclist but he was mostly cook and batman. Ever placid even under fire, he said simply: "It's that clown from the other outfit. He's chopping wood".

"What clown? And why is he chopping wood in our place?"

"Tain't his wood. It's ours."

"Oh, damn it, Michel, you never will explain! Fetch your clown and let's have a look at him."

The fellow sidled in, like a mongrel fearing another kick. He was flap-eared, pug-nosed, gap-toothed. His pants were too long, his sleeves too short. He looked sick, refused wine "because of my stomach", but accepted coffee. He crept nearer the fire as he drank. Then, sensing he was not going to be bullied, he told his story.

He was from the country, from Normandy. Farm life had no appeal. He tried several trades, then joined a travelling circus, "only a small one, no elephants and that sort of thing, but horses with girls who jump through hoops; and clowns, of

179

course." He did odd jobs until promoted to clowning. He must have been the one who always gets hit with the slapstick or the bladder, the dismal clown raising laughs at his own expense.

Whether in the tan-ring or in the Army he remained a butt. He did not get on well with his fellows. "You see, I'm a sick man. I've got flat feet, piles too, and my digestion is all wrong. I don't drink or smoke or play cards. The corporal doesn't like me, nor the sergeant. So all the fatigues and dirty chores come my way. Whenever I can, I huddle in a corner. Then they say I'm trying to shirk. Some days ago I sneaked around here to see what you men were like. Michel was kind to me."

Michel interposed: "Oh shut up! He wanted me to sell him some chocolate because he thought it'd do him more good than beef stew. I told him I didn't sell chocolate, but he could have some for nothing. So he comes here when he can and we make him welcome. He's been chopping wood for us, just to show he isn't a sponger."

"That's right," approved the man.

No one knew his name. Everyone called him the Clown. We became accustomed to seeing him around. One day he failed to come; his unit had been relieved. A week later it was our turn. Our destination was a village called Manheulles. Michel went ahead with the billeting party. He was waiting when we arrived in the middle of the night.

"What's this place like, Michel?"

"Much like any other, possibly worse. In any case it isn't cheerful. You've heard of men being 'shot at dawn'? Well, that's what's going to happen to Clown."

"Good God! What for?"

"So far as we can understand he's to be an example for the rest of us."

This was the story: two days before being relieved, Clown had been ordered to carry a message to the lines. He had pleaded that it was not his turn, then that he was ill. The corporal retorted that his name did not figure on the sick-list. The corporal was curt. Clown was sullen. Nobody quite knew what words were passed, but Clown was reported.

Some days later he came before a summary court-martial; his judges were officers of his own battalion. They sat in the school-house. It was all very short, for the case appeared very simple. The prisoner had been ordered to do something and had refused. His corporal had reported him. The report, in the usual way, had gone step by step to divisional headquarters. The general had returned it with instructions that the man should be tried – as an example. And there he was.

A young private who had read law was assigned to defend Clown. But that private belonged to the same battalion as the court; whatever the issue, they would meet again. He did his best, considering the limitations. He pleaded pathetically: "May it not be that the corporal misunderstood? May not the prisoner have said merely: 'I cannot' and not 'I will not?'" All to no purpose. The court filed out to consider its decision. It filed back to say: "Guilty". For "refusal to obey before the enemy" the only possible penalty was death. The prisoner was stunned; so were the men in the school-house.

There could be no appeal. Early in the war, a Presidential decree had "suspended temporarily the faculty of appealing against sentences passed by court-martial". Moreover, this was a drum-head court, authorised to sit "in special cases". The general therefore ordered the execution to proceed. His name was Butcher. Fate has such ironies!

Clown, meanwhile, had been lodged in the village lock-up, under strong guard. No one was permitted to see him, except a priest. His unit had none, so the Dominican monk whom mobilisation had brought to our battalion ministered to him.

When day dawned there passed through the village a sight that to this day must haunt all who saw it. Behind the firing squad came Clown. Supporting him with one arm, the monk strove to keep his eyes fixed on the crucifix held aloft in the other. More armed men followed. The only sound was shuffling feet. Villagers bared their heads; women crossed themselves.

The party passed from view, turned into a meadow. A volley. An example had been made!

They buried Clown in the village cemetery, but not in the same row as comrades killed in action. He must be an example even in death. Yet it was noted later that when soldiers brought humble flowers the unmarked grave was not overlooked. In 1916 came the attack on Verdun. Manheulles was taken by the Germans. Month after month it was pounded by shells until nothing was left standing. And when American infantry entered the village, a few days before the Armistice, the bodies of Clown and the others had returned to one and the same dust.

Had Clown been an isolated instance, it would have been none the less deplorable. It was not. So numerous indeed did "examples" become that opinion was alarmed, both at the front and in the rear. Worse, it was learned that, in some cases, there had not even been a semblance of a trial, only summary execution. Indignation grew. In 1916 drum-head courts were abolished. Next the faculty of appeal was restored, after having been suspended "temporarily" for three years. But many minds remained deeply impressed, mine for one, and the thought persisted that sometimes when a superior fails to obtain obedience from subordinates it may be that his methods are wrong.

Some sentences became notorious. In April 1915 at Flirey a company of the 63rd Infantry showed no enthusiasm to renew an attack which had signally failed two weeks before. The names of six men were drawn by lot – to be shot. In much the same circumstances, at Souain, four corporals of the 336th Infantry were executed; one of them, Maupas, a school-teacher, was forty-five years old. Six men of the 298th Infantry met the same fate at Vingré. Some subaltern officers also were executed – no generals.

Nor were "examples" limited to soldiers. Four members of one family were convicted in 1914 of "flashing information to the enemy". Father and mother died in prison. The damning evidence against them was possession of a lantern marked "Made in Germany". They had been denounced by a neighbour. Another man was shot because when a shell wrecked the coop his pigeons "flew off towards the German lines".

On November 24, 1941, the following letter was written by the then Minister of War, Louis Barthou, to the widow of an officer of the 347th Infantry, who had been executed without trial by "superior order":
    "Madam, the testimony produced in the course of a recent suit brought by you against a Paris newspaper made it a duty for me to examine anew the appeal you have addressed on several occasions to my predecessors and myself. The outcome of this examination, as also of previous documents, is that your husband, Lieutenant Herduin, was executed without trial forty-

eight hours after he fell back from Douaumont to Verdun, June 11, 1916. If an impartial appreciation of this painful fact is to be made, it cannot be separated from those tragic hours when the fate of France was linked to a victory at Verdun; yet it occurred only because of erroneous application of Regulations. Your husband, who had a very good record and who received the Military Medal during the war, was a gallant officer whose name your son and yourself may bear with honour. The law does not permit revision of his case, but the Government has decided, on my proposition, to grant you the sum of 100 000 francs as civil reparation."

At that time 100 000 francs represented about $7, 000. "Erroneous application of Regulations". What a euphemism! "The law does not permit revision." That was the very point which troubled so many plain men, who imagined that power to make laws implied power to unmake them if necessary. Why this confession of impotence, asked thousands who had been through the war? They set out to stir public opinion and there was formed a National Committee for the Rehabilitation of Men Shot by Order of Court-martial. The very name is a reflection on civilisation. Finally, in 1932, fourteen years after the Armistice, there was instituted a Court of Military Justice to revise "erroneous applications of Regulations". It consisted of three magistrates from civil courts and four war veterans, a composition marking a significant departure in French judicial methods.

This Court revised many judgments, rehabilitated many memories. In the case of the "four corporals of Souain" its decision contained the following pregnant passage: "it is clearly shown by the evidence that the attacks ordered were not realisable; they were destined to remain without result and to send to their death all those who left the trench".

In all logic the consequence should have been the reform of a system which, even if the slate were wiped clear as regards those who gave such orders, permitted them to be given. Instead, the law on court-martial was amended in a more humane and democratic sense. Now the judges include a private soldier and provision is made for adequate defence of the accused. Whereas formerly he was represented merely by a soldier or an officer assigned by his superiors, today there is a Corps of Defenders, all attorneys beyond the age for active service. Holding rank of captain, they are in a position to demand observance of legal forms. This is a gain, evidently, but it leaves the major problem as before.

Sad as were all these facts, sadder still is the impression that circumstances may arise in a democratic civilisation when the individual remains utterly helpless to prevent what manifestly should not be. To me the case of Clown was a great blow; it sapped the foundations of philosophical and political beliefs. Obviously the shooting was not only an erroneous but an immoral application of Regulations. Yet any objector would have been powerless; possibly he would have met a similar fate. No doubt at every rung of the ladder, from corporal to general, each truly believed he was performing his duty. Possibly all were honest and humane in the ordinary course of life, but here they were cogs in a machine. They were convinced that they were applying what made the machine work. And since machines have no hearts, they were heartless too. So Clown went to his death with men about him raging inwardly, gritting their teeth at their impotence to prevent a man-made monster from devouring other men.

The rage was all the deeper in the case of those who discerned that the solution did not lie in giving the machine a new cog, but a soul. Otherwise, only when it is all over, when wrongs have been done, is it possible to intervene.

185

Rehabilitation is laudable; prevention is preferable. All of which is duly accepted in theory and denied in practise. Despite all reforms and all modifications, despite the fact that in 1939-40 the new system was not only in application but widely presented as a democratic triumph, the instant the crisis developed in May everything went by the board. Summary courts were re-established and the faculty to appeal was suspended. There is every reason to believe, however, that no "examples" were made this time – if only because military courts were the first to beat a retreat!

Impotence, moreover, is not confined to individuals; there is the impotence of groups, of leaders even. We have seen how in 1917 Nivelle obstinately insisted on launching his offensive although the conditions on which his plan had been based had changed fundamentally. Even the generals entrusted with its execution had lost faith. The plan was being discussed openly at every street corner. Things reached such a point that General Lyautey, summoned post-haste from Morocco to become Minister of War, demanded communication of Nivelle's plan.

It was brought him by Colonel Georges Renouard, Head of the Operations Section at G.H.Q., who had served under his orders in Africa. The scene was described later by Lyautey himself. As the colonel spoke, the Minister pressed for his personal opinion, but he feigned not to hear.

Then Lyautey: "Renouard! I want an answer. Forget that I am Minister of War, forget that you are a colonel. We are two Frenchmen, face to face, and the fate of France is at stake. What do you think of the plan you have brought me?"
"Sir", came the reply, "I do not consider that I am called upon to express any opinion. I am General Nivelle's subordinate and mouthpiece; I have no right to pass judgment on my chief."

Lyautey took him by the shoulders, saying: "Look me straight in the eye, Georges. Imagine yourself back in Morocco when you had my full confidence. What do you really think of this?"

With welling tears the colonel said: "General, your opinion is mine; this plan is sheer madness."

Thereupon Lyautey hastened to Aristide Briand, then Prime Minister, and demanded that Nivelle should be removed. Briand replied that the conduct of operations was not within the province of the Minister of War. Soon afterwards an incident in the Chamber of Deputies provoked Lyautey's resignation, which, in its turn, involved that of the whole Cabinet. Paul Painlevé became Minister of War. He also had doubts about the feasibility of Nivelle's plan. For days there were conferences and negotiations among the highest personages in the land, both civil and military. Not, mind you, to consider a change of commander-in-chief or to cancel the offensive, but to make it appear that there was unanimity and that the machine was intact. The upshot was that on the morning of April 16, in a blizzard, the French began an attack doomed to failure by general consent. Between breakfast and lunch 30 000 men had been killed – one hundred and sixty a minute! Some days afterwards as the survivors were driven in trucks to rest billets, they shouted: "Long live peace!" and "We were led to slaughter!"

In the present war also there was at least one instance of collective impotence. General Maurice Gamelin had been set on a pinnacle, chiefly by those whose purposes he served. When the campaign developed in Norway, governing circles turned to him. What was his opinion? What did he intend to do? What were the chances of success? As imperturbable as Nivelle in 1917 – and as stubborn – he replied merely that his staff had

187

long been working on his plans and that everything had been foreseen – first day after zero hour, tenth day, fifteenth day, and so on. The scene has been described by a witness who subsequently held Cabinet rank in "the French Government installed in Vichy". Those who heard Gamelin speak thus were by no means reassured; indeed they were struck dumb. But they were impotent, except in one particular – they could remove Gamelin. But who was prepared to take the responsibility?

But what of America in all this? At the front during the First World War it seemed more distant than ever. What little news reached was printed in papers strictly censored to conform with official views and policies – the views and policies of the machine, heartless and soulless. Nevertheless, at the front, we were stirred when we heard of volunteers who had enlisted in the Foreign Legion, of Alan Seeger's rendez-vous with Death, of the exploits of the La Fayette Flying Corps. We had occasion also to see the boys of the American Field Service at work, removing our wounded in their ambulances, even under fire. We were excited indeed when Germany's submarine warfare led to breaking of relations. And the whole front cheered when a few weeks later America entered the war. We felt instinctively that it marked a turning-point in the history of Europe.

So far as I was concerned, my decision was immediate. On April 7, 1917, as soon as the momentous news reached the front, I made formal application to be transferred to some position, any position, with the American Expeditionary Force. As week after week passed, I realised that the application must have been stopped at some stage on the long road that separates a battalion post of command from G.H.Q.; someone must have said: "Why is he in such a hurry? Let him wait until G.H.Q. takes the initiative." That, of course, is the way they have in the Army.

It happened that sometime later our unit was attached to the 8th Army, then commanded by General Gérard. His political leanings were towards the Left, for which reason he was classified as a "Republican general". Soon he gave notice that, one day each week, he would receive the men under his command, whatever their rank. This was an innovation indeed. It was decried as demagogic by officers of the old school. That was sufficient for me to consider it democratic and I promptly solicited an audience. In due course I was summoned to Army Headquarters.

It was an interesting experience. Leaving the front-lines at dawn and driving some twenty miles in a supply wagon, I was the first arrival and my name consequently led the audience list. I was told to get something to eat and report again before two o'clock. When I returned the waiting-room was already filled with officers of all ranks and a sprinkling of sergeants and privates. While we waited a staff major entered the room, apparently seeking someone. His face seemed familiar; inquiry confirmed the fact. He was Paul Boncour, a rising star in the Socialist party, future Minister of Foreign Affairs and Prime Minister. The "Republican general" had taken him as one of his aids.

At two o'clock sharp, a door opened and an orderly appeared, list in hand. Senior officers prepared to be ushered into the general's presence. To their astonishment – and possible disgust – my name was called. Gérard rose to receive me, shook my hand, told me to be seated and asked my business. I explained that four months before – we were then in August – I had applied for service with the American Army, that I considered myself qualified by my knowledge of English and my long connection with the *New York Herald*. He assented. We spoke for some minutes of Bennett and newspapers generally. Then he dictated to a secretary: "The sergeant-major will renew his application, which I desire to be brought to my personal attention when it reaches Army Headquarters." Whereupon he rose, shook my hand again and I withdrew. It was all very pleasant and friendly and democratic. But the fact remains that it was not until December, another four months, before I was instructed to report to the French Military Mission attached to the American Expeditionary Force at Chaumont, where Pershing had established his G.H.Q. Evidently even a "Republican general" was powerless against the bureaucratic machine.

CHAPTER 13

THE YANKS ARE COMING!

"Formidable!" That was the popular reaction in France when the American Expeditionary Force began to arrive. "Formidable!" Had just come into colloquial vogue to denote astonished admiration. It well expressed the astonishment produced by the discovery of a very strange people. Stupendous, breath-taking, astounding, fantastic – "formidable" means all that. It means also: "Did you ever? Well, I never! Fancy that!" In former days, when English gentlemen made the "grand tour", their seeming eccentricities were dismissed with a shrug of the shoulders and a good-natured: "These mad English!" Now it became: "These mad Americans! They are formidable!" But such summary judgment has a great drawback; it does not invite comprehension.

Strange of speech and manner, strange in uniform and equipment, with funny hats and funnier packs, here were soldiers coming to war with toothbrushes, typewriters, toilet-paper, prophylactics. "Formidable!" In time they brought monster locomotives and equally monster trucks; equipment in unbelievable variety and quantity. They needed vast areas for their Services of Supplies, strung their own telephone lines, operated their own railroad trains, did everything on an unheard-of scale. And in their wake came welfare organisations, entertainers, lecturers, preachers. "Formidable!" The British had seemed queer enough. But these Americans!

These strange men were well received and soon made many friends. For one thing they had plenty of money and they were lavish with cigarettes of brands then unknown in France. They had winning ways; mothers beamed when some husky lad romped with their children, for all the world like a great St Bernard dog. In village billets these men shared their meals with the peasants, exchanging very white bread for very red wine. On their part, these young men found France a strange world. It was unavoidable that misconceptions should arise. One persists to this day – "the United States had to pay rent for the trenches in which our boys fought."

It would have been wise from the very outset if, as they arrived, a point had been made of explaining to these Americans many French ways and methods; it would have been wise also if bureaucracy had forgone much of its red tape. A capital mistake on the part of many was to consider the American Army merely as an adjunct to the French; it took them some time to realise that it was determined to remain always independently and autonomously American.

Bureaucrats immersed in routine expected to know that in France villagers are compelled to receive billeted troops and that in return these troops pay rent. Like much else in France the compensation is absurdly small: in 1917 the scale was twenty cents for an officer's bed "with sheets" and one cent for each man accommodated in a barn or loft. When horses were stabled the peasant had a right to the droppings! The system was applied automatically to the Americans. Billet lists were filled, the sums due were worked out – and the bill was presented to the Expeditionary Force. This was not done in any mercenary spirit, but just unthinkingly. It gave rise to a legend of rent for trenches, which lived long.

From the first, of course, French liaison officers were assigned to American units, but their province was essentially military. For the most part they were selected with judgment;

that they were tactful and efficient is proved by the fact that for years many of them continued to correspond with officers to whom they were attached. But liaison was not enough. There was great need for interpretation – interpretation of France to America and of America to France. As had been the case with the British Expeditionary Force, the French had recourse for this purpose to "auxiliary interpreters", soldiers whose chief qualification was knowledge of the English language. The British asked no more of these interpreters than to arrange billets, attend to relations with the civil authority, and frequently to assist also in running the officers' mess. Such duties were not exhausting; André Maurois, who was one of them, found time to write two books. Not so with the Americans. They wanted to know things. "How old is that church? What crop is growing in that field? What is your forestry system?" And so on – hundreds of questions in every field of human activity. This placed great responsibility upon the interpreter. He typified France in the eyes of the newcomers and on his presentation of France enduring judgment was likely to be passed.

It was a mistake to suppose, therefore, that mere knowledge of English was the prime qualification. Yet men were accepted haphazard for this vital task of creating first impressions. It was not until October 1917 that it was decided to establish a training centre for interpreters. Then things changed. All sorts of applicants were received – bankers, artists, writers, lawyers, teachers, clerks, cooks, waiters, and butchers, bakers and candlestick-makers – examined, trained and eventually assigned to American units, not only for their knowledge of English but for their knowledge of life and of the world.

Evidently, in the eyes of the Staff, interpreters were an unavoidable nuisance. Why on earth could not Americans speak French? For months they were appointed with manifest reluctance, all the more so since most of them came from units at the front. No captain, no colonel ever wants to let one man go. Then, when American arrivals increased in numbers each week and interpreters became an imperative necessity, things went to the other extreme. Every applicant was despatched to the training centre without troubling to verify his qualifications. In 1917 it had taken eight months to consider my application, despite an audience with an army commander; in the spring of 1918 it was taking no more than a week. By that time I had been given a commission and was charged with the preliminary examination of candidates.

"Sir," said a new arrival, "I wish to make a clean breast of it. I know no English. I shall be punished, of course, but I want to make my position clear from the start."

"That's very proper and manly, but why on earth did you make an application?"

"Sir, you know Army methods. An order comes down to company or battery commanders to send names of men knowing engineering or dairy-farming or what not; in this case it was English. Then months pass before anything happens. I calculated that I should certainly have time to get a smattering of English before a decision was taken. I immediately sent to Paris for grammars and dictionaries. Lo and behold! I was transferred even before the books arrived!"

It turned out, however, that being considered an unavoidable nuisance was not without advantages. The training centre was located in a village considered conveniently distant from Pershing's headquarters at Chaumont. The French Mission there affected to regard it as really beneath its notice; just as there were dumps for munitions, this was a dump for interpreters, where they could wait until their services were needed. That condescending attitude was the making of the centre, which was able to work its own salvation without retarding routine, bureaucratic hindrance or invocation of precedents. It worked so well that General W.C. Neville testified: "I cannot express myself too warmly upon the favourable impression made upon me by the splendid gentlemen who acted as interpreters with the Marines".

This achievement was due to two factors: firstly, the spirit animating the instructors, not a few of whom had taught in American colleges; secondly, a deliberate departure from certain traditional Army practises, made possible only because the centre was content to remain a mere dump in name though not in reality. Having been improvised, there were many anomalies in the Corps of Interpreters. For example, each man – officers were not eligible – retained the rank he had held in the French Army. This was justice; stripes had been won on active service. Yet in a special formation with special duties it would have been wise to waive rules regarding promotion. Equality does not always make for efficiency. Dr Alexis Carrel had come from the Rockefeller Foundation to serve his country; in the world of science he was a figure, in the Army he was a private, second class, in the Medical Corps. At the training centre – Biesles was the name of the village – a first sergeant did not necessarily turn out to be a first-class interpreter; conversely there were privates better fitted to their new task than were some non-commissioned officers. None the less, in the matter of promotion, the privates remained governed by Regulations; in the French Army a man must rise successively from rank to rank.

Esprit de corps saved the situation at Biesles. It became the rule in the new unit to appraise the value of a man by his character and accomplishment, not by the number of stripes on his sleeve. Interpreters of merit but holding no rank had as subordinates, in their special duties, not only other privates but corporals and sergeants also. The latter invariably set the example of subordination, while the former never forgot their inferiority in the military hierarchy. It stands to the everlasting honour of the Corps of Interpreters with the American Expeditionary Force that such a reversal of the existing order was possible. In the eyes of traditionalists, of course, this was rank anarchy. At Biesles all interpreters messed together and shared the same billets. In the classes the same principle was applied. Many of the instructors were privates; their moral authority was never questioned by their pupils, ranking from corporals to first sergeants. Biesles in its way provided a lesson in democracy.

Classes, lectures, readings occupied several hours daily. In lighter vein there were debates, chorus singing, concerts, theatricals, reviews. Nor was physical training neglected. Baseball was taught and played with zest; there were field sports, cross-country runs, football games. And all this carried on in English and self–supporting; enough talent was discovered at the training centre to supply all its needs, from lecturers to baseball coaches. And there were no drills and no parades. Again rank anarchy!

A fair proportion of the men had lived in the United States; they helped to give Biesles that American atmosphere which was the main objective. Much was learned also form guest speakers from various welfare organisations. Biesles soon became American in its ways also, and one of its proudest achievements was the invention of a regular college yell complete with cheer-leader.

In this atmosphere the interpreters made rapid progress and revealed their individual temperaments, thus facilitating the task of assignment, which demanded much tact. Chaumont would telephone casually for interpreters of all kind – one of good presence and education for a divisional commander, another with a knowledge of surveying for a labour battalion, a third with a mathematical mind for an experimental anti-aircraft battery. Biesles was seldom at a loss. Very few proved unfit for their positions.

Yet the material was motley indeed, all sorts and conditions of men, including many a rough diamond. And the English of some was of the strangest. Moreover long months in the trenches had dulled many an intellect. Physical rest and mental relief soon set them right and after a little polishing most were fit for duty. Men returning from temporary assignments would tell of their experiences, notes would be compared, and it soon became evident that they had developed a proper understanding of the American character. But these interpreters necessarily remained a minority among the French.

The arrival of the American Expeditionary Force had been acclaimed with the deepest sincerity – a welcome prompted by many sentiments. One came from the heart. The doughboys were greeted as fellow-men who had come three thousand miles to help fight for universal liberty in the abstract, for French hearths and homes in the concrete. And the masses were drawn instinctively to this race which, descended from men who had left Europe to seek freedom across the seas, now returned for the sake of that very freedom. They called it democracy, but it was freedom they meant.

If emotionalism be a dominant trait in the American character, the French outvied them in emotion as the A.E.F. arrived. On occasion it verged on collective hysteria. They were stirring times, reminiscent of the early days of the Revolution, when hearts beat faster at the mere mention of liberty and brotherhood and unalterable friendship. There was a feeling in the very air that the end of the war would bring the Millennium. Pershing's "La Fayette, here we are!" had struck the keynote.

When Woodrow Wilson came for the peace negotiations he was literally worshipped. There is ever present in my mind's eye the scene at Biesles in 1918 when the President passed through at Christmastide after a tour of American camps and billets. No stop there was included in the program, but the interpreters were determined that there should be. At the crossroads in the centre of the beflagged village the interpreters waited nearly two hours. They numbered several hundred – the Armistice had brought many back from their units – supported by many villagers in their Sunday best. At last the Presidential automobile was sighted. It was compelled to halt by the crowd, which shouted, cheered, waved flags and handkerchieves, a mad milling mass weeping for joy, while loud above the din rose the Biesles yell: "Rah! Rah! Rah!"

Secret Service men jumped off the running boards with hand to hip. General John J. Pershing, who accompanied the President, was indeed "Black Jack" that minute, scowling and looking daggers. But Wilson understood and accepted the situation with a smile. He opened one door to listen to a short speech of greetings and signed the interpreters' golden book. Frenzied women showered him with flowers, while others kneeled in the mud literally to kiss the hem of his garment – a prosaic black coat. Was he not a saviour? At last "Black Jack" spoke: "And now may we proceed?" The car went on, pursued by another: "Rah! Rah! Rah!" Every time I met the General in after years I reminded him of the incident. He would laugh then.

In governing circles and by the High Command, the A.E.F. was sincerely welcomed also, for it came at a crucial moment. The threatened defection of Russia, following upon Nivelle's ill-starred and costly offensive had presented a dilemma: either attack the Germans before a total Russian collapse and without waiting for the Americans; or discount

Russian aid, await the Americans and be prepared to bear the brunt of German onslaughts. Painlevé, then Minister of War, wrote later: "On June 15 General Pershing arrived in Paris. In accord with General Foch, I asked him for one million American soldiers within a year. They were promised by July 1, 1918, with another million to follow, and still more if necessary. Both in France and in England there were only three men to believe this – General Foch, General Pétain and myself." The leaders chose the second course. The rest is history.

So that in all domains everything made for brotherly love. But, as it turned out, there was much talk, much oratory, but not enough striving after mutual comprehension. What responsible circles really needed was a corps of interpreters such as that trained at Biesles. Many a future misunderstanding would have been stifled at birth, many a difference killed in the germ. Take one instance, a speech that did incalculable harm.

It came from an expatriate American, Judge Walter Berry, a respectable gentleman who, through long residence abroad and many activities, had come to consider himself the mouthpiece of the American people. He had sat on the bench of the Mixed Courts in Egypt and had retained the judicial title despite his retirement. In the latter part of the war he was president of the American Chamber of Commerce in Paris, in which capacity he made the speech in question at the Washington Birthday dinner. In effect he addressed the French thus:

"You have been holding the fort for us. We shall not forget. Everything devastated in France we shall rebuild. We shall never ask for repayment of a cent. And even then we shall be in your debt."

Away from references I cannot give the exact words, but that was the gist.

I recall vividly the impression that pronouncement made. All the French newspapers gave it prominence as yet another token of Franco-American unity and solidarity, as a gesture that did not cause surprise from such a great and noble-minded people. When these papers reached the front several men came to me with happy faces. "The Americans have the right spirit" they said. "They're great!" How could they know, with none to tell them, that in the United States a chamber of commerce is purely a private organisation, whereas in France it is a semi-official body, under Government control. Even French officials accepted invitations to the Washington Birthday dinner under the impression that it was a solemn occasion where the views of the Government in Washington were echoed. And when the French masses read that Berry had spoken in the presence of the American Ambassador and several French Ministers how could they doubt that it was indeed the voice of America that they had heard? They little imagined that this was the beginning of a debt question destined to cast a shadow to this day over their relations with the United States.

This is not the place to analyse the military aspect of American participation in the First World War. We who mixed with American officers and men found them earnest and determined. They did not deny that they had much to learn, but they set out to learn it in their own way. They did not escape routine or red-tape, but it was their own routine and their own red-tape – which was another occasion for misunderstandings. My last vision of the A.E.F. in the field has been mentioned already, when a few days before the Armistice all roads leading to Lorraine bore day and night endless columns of large trucks bringing a mighty host for the battle set to open on November 14. Hundreds of trucks, and hundreds more, driven by small impassive Annamites and laden with thousands of husky, hard-jawed, grim-faced American men.

Foch refused to add to the long roll of dead and the war ended. Believing that it had been made safe for democracy, the world went wild on Armistice Day. In the Place de l'Opéra in Paris soldiers of many nations and a crowd of French men and women sang the "Marseillaise" and other anthems, cheered themselves hoarse, danced, kissed, laughed, wept and laughed again. The doughboys, "formidable" in this as in all else, gave Parisians their first taste of rip-roaring exuberance while women and girls singled them out for their kisses.

A new order had come. But soon the mirage faded. Twelve months later, on November 2, 1919, All Souls'day, I wrote in the *New York Herald*: "We can weep bitter tears for the dream that has failed, the lie that prevails, the war that prepares". Nor did I stand alone in my fears. There was no lack of pacifists and personally I had little faith in their efforts. Had I not been in close touch with two winners of the Nobel Peace Prize?

CHAPTER 14

HAIL COLUMBIA!

The decade immediately following the First World War, roughly from Armistice to Depression, was indeed an American era in France. It helped very much my quest.

The A.E.F. had brought many things in its train, including a stowaway in the form of the Colorado beetle, today still ravaging the potato fields of Europe. Some of those adopted forthwith by the French included jazz, cigarettes of "blond tobacco", horn-rimmed spectacles, chewing gum, a middle initial and safety razors. Others followed in due course. The logical French mind reasoned this – rather illogically: these people are "formidable" in every respect and they obtain "formidable" results; therefore let us copy them in every way. This admiration of American methods and American ways marked a turning point in French life, especially in the cities. So far as Paris is concerned, it was symbolised by the view on either side of the Concorde Bridge when facing the Madeleine. On the right the delicate spire of Sainte-Chapelle rose above the historic Cité, the Paris that developed between the Middle Ages and the 19th Century. On the left one saw another spire, that of the American Cathedral of the Holy Trinity, in the midst of 20th Century Paris, close to the Etoile, in the heart of the American section. So it was until the Depression. Then on the left there appeared the tower of another church, rebuilt St Pierre-de-Chaillot, of very modern concrete, quite dwarfing the American spire. Possibly that also was symbolical.

However that may be, the American craze extended well over ten years. Very soon it went beyond mere externals, such as the striped pole outside the barber shop, American dry cleaning, and so-called American bars. Not only was the name "building" adopted for business premises, but the offices they housed were equipped in American style and run on American lines. Taylorisation, assembly lines, mass production, sales talk and the like became current terms. The late Paul Dupuy asked me to plan an American copy desk for his *Petit Parisien*; the idea failed in the face of passive resistance from his executives. But they could not prevent French newspapers from adopting American make-up and banner headlines, while avidly purchasing features and comic strips of American origin. American influence was noted on all sides – shop-window displays, slogans, advertising methods, grapefruit and corn on the cob, cocktails and ice-cream-soda. And American films introduced into the language such words as gangster, racket, vamp and the now omnipresent "O.K."

True, the American craze extended also to other European countries, but in most cases circumstances were different. In Britain it was sponsored by those groups which insist that blood is thicker than water and whose motto is: "Hands across the sea". Moreover it was aided there by the common language. In Czechoslovakia, in Poland and some other countries it resulted from the contact with the homeland preserved by emigrants. In France none of these factors operated.

A strange point in this connection is that the French should have hailed as discoveries some things merely brought back to them in American guise. The explanation doubtless is that in the New World these things had become "formidable". Gangs and gangsters, rackets and racketeers, were nothing new in themselves; French history is filled with tales of the former while the latter, under the designation of "combine" and "combinard" permeated the whole of French life. In this land of

203

small jobs with small salaries there was not one, from Premiership to road sweeping, that was not eked out by a "combine". As for major scandals, whether financial or political, Heaven knows that France has had her full share of bribery and corruption. As for Tammany methods, they have not been confined to a mere city, however large, but have been practised for years throughout the length and breadth of the land – and by more than one party. But the craze was such that all these things were accepted as very novel and typically American.

Much of this Americanisation could be explained by the rush of tourists across the Atlantic that set in as soon as peace had been assured. In the main it was only skin-deep; and few troubled to probe further. The French accepted American tailoring, but cared little for the individuality beneath the clothes. As a consequence of utter misconception of the American character, it was imagined that there was no need to do more than treat the visitor as an overgrown child, fill his belly and tickle his vanity, to the accompaniment of interminable orations. The newspapers were filled with photographs and stories of "great friends of France"; junkets and joy-rides took them to every corner of the country, with unending dining and wining; decorations were distributed with a lavish hand. At the Invalides in Paris one-legged General Mariaux and one-armed General Gouraud were kept on constant duty pinning crosses of the Legion of Honour on manly American chests and buxom American bosoms. It was then a fond delusion at the Quai d'Orsay that ribbon, yards of it, eventually might balance the war debt. Those were the days when sentiment ran riot and La Fayette worked double-shifts. When disillusion came, Uncle Sam became "Uncle Shylock".

The American colony, permanent or transient, stood out among all others both as a favourite child and a chartered libertine. With the Ambassador, Myron T. Herrick, as "the greatest of the friends of France", the slightest American wish was gratified instantly – audiences with the President of the Republic, attendance of Cabinet Ministers at luncheon clubs, permission for the colour guard of the American Legion to attend ceremonies in uniform. Quick and easy Paris divorces for Americans developed into a scandal. Policemen only smiled when roisterers or brawlers showed an American passport; if they saw fit to climb the rails of Cluny Museum in order to sleep it off on the grass, it was reckoned merely an over-abundance of animal spirits.

No one, not even in the highest and consequently most responsible spheres, ever bothered to inquire into American ways. In Paris there was an American Club, a weekly luncheon gathering of businessmen, held in some restaurant since there was no club-house. It invited prominent men as guest speakers and the speeches were usually reported in the press. As a consequence, the name of the organisation was quite familiar to the French, though not its nature. In the popular view it came to mean something "formidable" among clubs. On one occasion while he was Premier, André Tardieu spoke there; a Left paper commented unfavourably on his "aristocratic relations"!

The culmination of this period came in 1927 when the Paris Convention of the American Legion accompanied a parade down the Champ-Elysées. At a banquet given the Legionnaires by the French Government, Raymond Poincaré, then Premier, delivered a set oration rather on the dull side. Foch was there, but did not figure on the list of speakers. He had finished his ice-cream, smacking his lips on his last spoonful, when the Americans clamoured for a speech. He rose with all the old vigour, pointed his spoon at an imaginary enemy, and spoke earnest, prophetic words. The theme was: 'Beware, be vigilant, the future is dark". He, at any rate, had never varied: "If the left bank of the Rhine is not French, it will mean another war".

In this factitious atmosphere, recalls to reality come as jolts. The refusal of the United States Senate to countenance the Treaty of Versailles had been a hard blow, all the harder since France had been led to assume – with the aid of the censor – that the entire nation was behind Wilson. Another was administered over the debt question. In their candour many Frenchmen had pinned their faith on Judge Berry and other amiable irresponsibles. On both issues they felt that they had been deceived.

During this period circumstances favoured my exploration. I returned to the *Herald* on demobilisation. There no longer being a Bennett on whom to dance attendance – he died in May 1918 – I took charge of the news department, this time with a staff almost entirely American. Several men had been with the A.E.F.; indeed some still wore uniform. Round the copy desk sat Harold Stearns, nursing his Bohemian spleen and meditating on the America he later rediscovered; Ralph Heinzen and William Hillman, destined to make their mark in news agencies; several others whose names are now well-known.

Most of the pre-war generation had drifted to other parts. In 1914, when the Germans threatened Paris, the then editor-in-charge, William L. Warden, at the head of a delegation, had waited upon the Commodore and urged him to transfer the paper to Bordeaux whereto the French Government had gone. (Warden died in 1942 after a very successful career with Lord Rothermere on the London *Daily Mail*; both affected the same Napoleonic forelock.) Bennett indignantly refused. Whatever his faults, he had guts. Instead of fleeing he, a septuagenarian, chose that precise moment to announce his marriage. Most of the delegation left for England and during the war the paper carried on with more or less scratch crews.

It was in the normal order of things that the policy of the paper should change also. When the A.E.F. arrived its circulation increased greatly and of necessity it had become much more American and much less cosmopolitan. That trend continued. Personally it offered me opportunity for many new contacts with things American. The time was particularly interesting. Paris had become the happy hunting ground of Young America and Montparnasse was its centre. Montparnasse became truly cosmopolitan; if Americans did not predominate in numbers, they certainly had a very marked influence there. Regardless of nationality, the new denizens differed entirely from those before the war. In the great majority they had not come to learn from Paris on classic lines; their purpose was to revolutionise those lines and to impose them on Paris. What became known as the Paris School of painting was represented mostly by aliens. Cubism, Dadaism, Surrealism, many other "isms" were essentially of Montparnasse, which became the home of all that was extreme either in art or literature. What a distance had been travelled since the early 19th Century, when the son of Albert Gallaton, then United States Minister, caused a scandal by posing as Cupid for a painting by David, that frigid classicist!

Painters and pseudo-painters gathered at Montparnasse from all points of the compass, some to work, some to idle, all to eat, drink and be merry. This was the time when money ran like water, when many an artist used more alcohol than paint, many a writer more drink than ink; when models, more or less nude, were more famous than those who painted them; when Montparnasse set out to outdo Montmartre, Greenwich Village and Chelsea combined to become the capital of world Bohemia. Jules Pascin was one of its bright particular stars. Although he was living in Montmartre when he killed himself in 1930 at the age of 45, he was a true Montparnassian. The cosmopolitan aspect of the place was well exemplified in his person. Born in Bulgaria (Julius Pinsca), his Jewish forebears having been Austrian, Romanian and Spanish, he died a naturalised American citizen.

Pascin worked hard in his way, but without method or continuity. And he drank harder. He was one of the founders of the ultra-modern Paris school and he made much money, in millions. At his parties hundreds of guests – with a preponderance of the uninvited - crowded the studio-apartment, in each room of which there was a table laden with solid and liquid refreshment. As one group left another took its place until all the liquor was absorbed. Pascin the while, drunk as a lord, stumbled from room to room, shouting that more drink be brought. He took his life because he was weary of everything, weary especially of painting. He died at a time when money was becoming scarce in Montparnasse, with the consequence that the variegated crowd there began to be weary of drinking. It ended by putting much water into its liquor.

Of the painters and writers of Montparnasse during that decade there were two kinds – the anarchist and the plodder. The anarchists ever sought something new, especially the bizarre and the extravagant. To succeed in their quest they needed new sensations, with liquor and noise, always more liquor and always more noise. The successful anarchists made much money while their vogue lasted. The unsuccessful passed their time cadging the price of a meal or a drink. At heart the anarchists were disgusted with themselves, as Pascin was. The plodder was not disgusted with himself, but he was beginning to wonder whether he was not disgusted with Montparnasse, the boundaries of which are an allegory in themselves – a railroad terminal at one end and a cemetery at the other! How could he plod in all that din and trepidation?

Reversing the situation before the war, there were now more American writers than painters in Montparnasse. Most of them came really to work, if also to experiment – in style, in presentation, in typography even. Some came because America disappointed their yearnings, some to flee Prohibition. On the whole the experimenters outnumbered the iconoclasts – all were animated by unbounded enthusiasm. Not only did they write prose or verse, but they launched vanguard magazines and reviews, printed their works on hand-presses, set themselves up as booksellers and publishers. There were experimenters in music and in photography; and they investigated many possibilities – which remained possibilities.

Thanks to my work on the *Herald* I saw much of the early phase of the American invasion which set in just after the war. The vanguard was composed of scores of correspondents who came to report negotiations for peace. Then began the westward flow of European news which since then has increased steadily year by year. In 1914 there were about twelve full-time correspondents in Europe; by 1939 they numbered nearly 800. Never had the world seen such an assemblage as the Peace Conference in Paris – innumerable delegations, councils, commissions and sub-commissions, committees and sub-committees. Never had there been such disputes, bickerings, hagglings, intrigues, test balloons. Never, furthermore, had there been such a disappointment for those who set their faith on liberty and democracy. From the start the Great Powers which had convened the Conference made it clear that their part therein was to be arbitrary and dictatorial.

Many an echo from the council chambers – of eloquent platitudes, of displays of crass ignorance, of animus, vanity, passion, threats and counter-threats. In the intervals between fights behind closed doors the world was told in florid phrase that all was going well and that the future of Humanity was in good hands. Propaganda ran wild. And, to cap all, the Censor was even more despotic than during the war. Out of all this turmoil came the Treaty of Versailles and the Covenant of the League of Nations, doomed to failure from the very day of signature. During four years or more, men had been told that they were fighting for Right and Justice; more specifically, that the object of the war was "to make the world a decent place to live in". The sum and total of it all seemed to be that nothing had changed, except for more words, more taxes, more promises unfulfilled. No venture was possible, for no one knew what the morrow might bring forth. The "Mad Twenties" resulted.

One revelation of the Peace Conference was the extent to which the United States had organised publicity in every sphere, especially communication between government and people through the press. Whereas, with the possible exception of Britain, the European system was still to issue "official communiqués" saying nothing in many words, and printed perfunctorily in the papers, the Americans had progressed exceedingly – press officers, press conferences with the privilege of putting questions, and every facility for direct contact with leaders. It was realised that industry and commerce were far ahead of Europe in the matter of press agents and press relations generally. True, skeptics argued that it was only a disguised way of making use of the press. Nevertheless, at the worst there was a semblance of keeping the people informed; moreover frequently news actually was given.

In the midst of this post-war agitation the *Herald* changed hands. Thanks to the A.E.F. the Paris edition had been prospering but in New York the outlook was dark. The paper there was drifting; its policies had become out-dated and out-moded and there was no one to take the helm with adequate authority. Early in 1920 an announcement was cabled us for publication informing the world that Frank A. Munsey was our new publisher. The Paris *Herald* was allowed to go on in the old way, but gradually changes were made. Bennett was derided as a back number, his cosmopolitan appeal was abandoned and the *Herald* set out to be "an American paper for Americans". (Soon thereafter it was realised that Bennett was "not so dumb" and that there was much method in his madness – but too late). The challenge was met by the European edition of the *Chicago Tribune* – now but a memory – which gloried each day in its front page that it was the only American paper in Europe edited by Americans. I was retained as managing editor, doubtless because of my experience, since Munsey used to boast that "he didn't have to bother about his European edition; it run itself". Yet it became manifest that my nationality was against me in the new order. I remained four years notwithstanding.

Compared with Bennett days, the situation was reversed. We saw little of Munsey; the fact that he had become publisher was made evident by pronouncements over his signature cabled for publication on the front page of a paper in which Bennett's name had appeared only at his death. Stories circulated on Munsey's harsh domination, tempered by no redeeming traits. When he did come to Paris the atmosphere was frigid. On the occasion of his first visit the executives were invited to meet him at luncheon. No sooner were we seated that he drew a clipping from his vest pocket with the cheering remark: "Someone's going to be fired for this". An error had crept into a despatch from New York relating to "my friend Samuel Untermyer". I took full responsibility and no one was fired. But the impression was ghastly. In revenge, Munsey became known amongst us as "The Grocer".

It may be recalled – or it may not – that in addition to his papers and magazines, Munsey was interested in a chain of grocery stores. One day in my presence he was introduced to a French publisher not only as a newspaper magnate but as "a successful grocer". The idea was to magnify his qualities as a businessman. The Frenchman was taken aback, and no wonder since in France "épicier" is used as a term of derision for hacks whose literary productions are fit only to wrap groceries. I hastened to explain that in "Monsieur Munsey's case 'épicier' was an understatement; he was in reality director of a large provision business with many branches". This interpretation relieved the situation. But the story went the rounds. The staff adopted with glee doggerel which a copy-reader discovered in some magazine or other:

> "The grocer who has made his pile,
> Does he grow nicer? No, Sir.
> He does not change his heart or style,
> But becomes a grosser grocer."

Working for our grosser grocer became less and less congenial. Finally I resigned in 1924 to launch an afternoon paper *The Paris Times*. My four years with Munsey had not been lost; through him and his entourage I had been able to study a type of American previously unknown to me.

I had met the shrewd New Englander, but I had yet to make the acquaintance of a real "slick Yank". Munsey and his methods served to complete my collection. Of course, we all know that sentiment has no place in business; in his case there was no sentiment even out of business, or more correctly perhaps everything was business to him. Bennett certainly was wrapped in self, but he had moments of expansion when he became human; also he could laugh. Munsey, cold, calculating, always seemed to be meditating a deal. He would say: "I generally fall on my feet". That summed him up. To fall on his feet with the Paris *Herald* he had to abandon some of that hundred per cent Americanism advertised initially. During the interminable discussions arising from the application of the Treaty of Versailles he frequently opposed the French view. That provoked talk of his being pro-German, which did not help to do business in Paris. So two sets of reports were written, one to be cabled for American consumption, the other for publication in the European edition.

The Depression changed many things. In particular it thinned the ranks of the expatriates. Much of things American had been learned from the humbler class of tourists, attracted by cheap steamship rates. But by the time Franklin Roosevelt devalued the dollar the golden age of American travel had passed. In the meantime the prodigal had learned thrift. When the flow came again, though much reduced, he expected full value for his money. On their part, the French also had learned; they had come to a more sedate appreciation of the American character. No longer did they believe in a legendary figure raining gold with double-fisted generosity. America also was off gold!

In point of fact, in those ten or twelve years an error in psychology was permissible. For the most part the American tourist of that period was new to European travel. His timidity triumphed over his shrewdness. He became an easy prey and his all-pervasive smile was interpreted to mean he liked it. He did not. So that, even before the Depression, either he stayed at home or travelled elsewhere. The resultant wreckage was seen in the list of bankrupt hotels and closed restaurants; finished was the spontaneous generation of night-clubs for harvesting American dollars. And the price of champagne ebbed when it could be drunk lawfully on the other side of the Atlantic. So it

213

was at Montparnasse, too, where the disillusioned American intellectual no longer brought prosperity to notorious haunts.

The Americans who came to Montparnasse after the dollar went off gold included no would-be Pascins. They came to paint, to write or to dream away the hours, each according to his bent. But many more came specifically to compute the possibilities of the Roosevelt dollar in terms of the Blum franc. This was their second monetary experiment; previously they had exhausted the purchasing power of the Poincaré franc. Mindful of currency exchange, they were wary. In so doing they were like the natives. The Carrefour Vavin abandoned pyrotechnics; even such a Latin Quarter celebrity as Kiki, the model, looked after the pennies.

The newly arrived or newly-returned expatriates, having rediscovered Greeley at home, began migration westward. From Montparnasse they trekked to Vaugirard, where the lowing of kine in freight trains passing over the "Bridge of the Beeves" bound for the abattoirs, mingled strangely with jazz hot from transatlantic gramophones. Here the expatriate hauled home each morning a string-bag from the open-air market where, among jostling housewives, he learned the art of making both ends meet. Probably it was the best way of appreciating the character of the people. Conversely, it made the French realise that all Americans are not millionaires, that they should be considered as fellow humans and no longer as money-bags. Devaluation tended to make the whole world kin and Franco-American relations gained in consequence.

Gone were the days of Judge Walter Berry, gone never to return. That Fourth of July oration, when he magnanimously pledged the United States never to claim its debt, had made his relations with the French even more extensive and cordial than before. Marcel Proust had written to him in all seriousness: "If it (the World War) can go on all right, we owe it to the Americans set in motion by Walter Berry". In another letter he referred to Berry as "one of two or three men I love best in the world". Which meant just nothing to France and America, certainly nothing to Proust, although Berry lapped it up avidly.

Yet traditions are hard-lived. Even during the present war there were inconsiderate pronouncements by irresponsible speakers among expatriates, even among some holding official positions. Draped in highfalutin, replete with allusions to Democracy and Freedom, they tended to instill the idea of eventual American participation. Which may explain in part why Paul Reynaud, in those tragic days of June 1940 saw fit to invoke immediate American aid if France were to resist further.

All that past is dead and done with. The last survivor of a glamorous age, Evander Berry Wall, passed away while the outcome of the war was still in suspense. In France he played the part of the last of the dandies. New York was no longer the place for descendants of Beau Brummel, whereas it was so easy – with money, a four-in-hand tie and a Chow dog – to become "the most Parisian of Americans". Draw the curtain; values have changed, for war has come anew. And the cinematograph reel unwinds again after an intermission of twenty years.

CHAPTER 15

THAT FUNNY WAR

Twenty years may change history; they do not change man. The "war to end war" begins again. Once more millions of men open their Army books and wonder why. Czechoslovakia, Poland, mean little to them. Regardless of what the newspapers may say, they do not consider themselves Crusaders for the Right or Champions of Democracy. All they know is that this is the third scare – and the second mobilisation – in a twelvemonth: too much for plain peaceful people to bear. "Il faut en finir" placidly quotes Neville Chamberlain. Nevertheless they are stunned by the realisation that for twenty years all the talk has been of peace, only to end in war. There are no shouts this time, no songs, only apathetic impotence.

Long trains bear men eastward again. Most of them are sons of those who left in 1914; some, however, are to be blooded for the second time. Many of these are subaltern officers in the Reserve. Imagining that nothing has changed, they recall how they went "over the top" and "crawled through a barrage". One thing is new nevertheless: they do not say that they are bound for the front, but that they are going to the Maginot Line. Soon it is just "The Line". And on "The Line" Hitler will break his teeth. Moreover the English, this time, are already in the field and unity of command is assured. In the other war it took three years to reach unity.

Otherwise it is the same old story – regiments formed laboriously, more laboriously even, since the proportion of reservists is greater; much fussing, much cursing – then, into the fray.

The Germans being busy in Poland, we march resolutely towards the Westwall. Soon the frontier is crossed. Hurrah! All is well. This time there will be no invasion of French soil. Yet the advance is far from easy. The enemy infantry is forced back, it is true, but it is evident that equipment is to play its part in this war. The ground is strewn with land-mines – three thousand in Warndt Forest alone. Citations published later tell the tale. But never mind the cost. Push on from the Moselle to Lauterburg! Soon the outworks of the Westwall are reached. Hurrah!

Meantime soldiers posted along the Rhine write of days of peace and plenty. The Germans have not fired a shot. "The villagers having been evacuated, we are living on the fat of the land. Poultry and roast pork galore. Many of us sleep in beds. T'is a strange war!"

T'is a strange war indeed. Soon the advance halts. For strategic reasons of course, though some shake their heads and speak of lack of heavy guns. The troops fall back to the frontier, but "The Line" is behind them – and Hitler will break his teeth on it someday.

Meantime the strange war is becoming stranger. On each side there are tanks, machine-guns, airplanes, cannon, modern engines of war of every kind, yet the fighting is now hand-to-hand. The battlefield is reduced to a strip of no man's land in which patrols constantly skirmish. They are armed with knives and bludgeons and have dogs with them. They creep through the night like Indian braves on the war-path; and when ten men meet ten other men the encounter figures in the communiqué.

217

Newspaper correspondents are allowed to go to the front, and I am of the number. In duty bound they magnify each skirmish, for there is nothing else. They are taken to see works of the Maginot Line, which they describe with a wealth of superlatives. Rightly so, for these warships embedded in the earth are truly remarkable, and every day more obstacles and more defences are being built – tank traps, abatis, gun emplacements, water lines, entanglements. Let Hitler come and he will see. Time is working for us. Why doesn't the fool come now?

There are relatively few men on "The Line". The others just wait until the Germans decide to come and be killed. Waiting is dreary and the troops must be occupied. "Social sections" are created for all large units and everywhere talk runs on football, games, books, radio sets, cinema shows, all possible forms of recreation and entertainment. On its part, the Government, sensing that the men are wondering why they could not just as well play cards at home, grants mass furloughs and distributes medals with lavish hand. "Sightseeing circuits" are organised for war correspondents and distinguished visitors, all of whom return with collections of regimental badges. Each unit is encouraged to devise an emblem – pretty things with bright and coloured enamel. And there are regimental newspapers, some with coloured strips and Sunday sections all complete. Yes, a strange war! Comforts aplenty are sent to the front. In particular there is much comfort in liquid form. At Christmas the troops quaff "Daladier champagne". Good for Edouard!

Winter sets in with rigour. It is a severe test for it has taken the Quartermaster Corps by surprise. Blankets lack, warm garments also. In billets there is plenty of fuel, and the men do not suffer unduly. But at the outposts the misery is complete, cruel. Bread freezes in the sling-bag, wine in the canteen. No water, no fire – enemy watchers would spot it. And since the Germans simply won't attack, Indian warfare must continue, even in the snow. Patrols now go out in white overalls.

Periodically there is an operation on a large scale – a company, even a battalion. It may herald real war. For two days everyone is on the alert. But soon the front reverts to the old routine.

One outcome of the long wait is an avalanche of paper. Staffs have grown plethoric, what with "social sections" and press officers and peddlers of football and crime stories. Everywhere have sprung up repair shops and supply centres, dumps and parks of all kinds, canteens and cooperative stores, all seemed designed to last. Some officers and men do sterling work, some hold sinecures, but all have this in common – to justify their existence they have to draft reports and prepare graphs and statistics. Nothing is more contagious.

In a sector on the Rhine, near Strasburg, a colonel tells me: "I sleep seven hours; two hours for meals, seven to inspect the defences. That leaves eight, all taken up in reading, writing and annotating reports." He spoke on a village street upon returning from a visit to pill-boxes on the river bank. As an officer emerged from the command post, he continued: "No Captain, I am not coming in now! I shall have supper first, otherwise I would be scribbling and signing for the next two hours."

Months go by. Spring comes. The strange war continues. The Germans simply will not attack. Can't they understand the dolts, that time is working against them? Don't they know it's a blockade? Occasionally there are alarms. The enemy seems to be preparing an offensive – through Holland, or through Belgium, or through Switzerland. After several days of anxiety nothing comes of it. The wait is renewed.

Much has been done to strengthen the Maginot Line, and fieldworks have prolonged it from Montmédy to the North Sea. Gamelin proclaims that all this is "formidable" – blessed word. Daladier says triumphantly: "Our losses scarcely exceed one thousand." Under these conditions why worry? Let's play football until Hitler does attack.

In their leisure moments the men read much – books, newspapers, reviews. Constantly they ask for more. Visiting defences North of Maubeuge I am accompanied by a captain who, in normal life, is a prosperous banker. (The day before my guide was a member of the exclusive Jockey Club. Why are press officers all of one class?). In our automobile, my feet rest on a bundle of back numbers of the *Revue des Deux Mondes*, world-renowned, estimable, but caviar to the general. Since there is deep snow everywhere, I assume that the bundle is purely utilitarian.

We stop at a casemate on a road close to the Belgian border, where a lieutenant has charge of thirty men, rugged sons of the soil, never relieved. There is evidence that their welfare has his earnest attention. He suggests that reading matter would be welcome, which reminds the banker-captain of my footstool. The lieutenant recognises the salmon-pink covers and starts. Dutifully, he restrains himself and even murmurs thanks.

I take him aside and promise that on my return to Paris I shall send him what he really wants. I keep my promise – Jules Verne, Alexandre Dumas, Pierre Benoît, popular magazines. He acknowledges receipt with effusive thanks, and tells me that in the interval he has been promoted captain. I sense that should the banker visit again there will be talk from man to man.

From current publications those at the front learn that Germany is in sorry plight – plenty of men, it is true, but many of them untrained; the same with subaltern officers. Railroads have no rolling stock and the tracks are in bad condition. There is scarcity of food, of clothing, of everything. At the first military setback the whole structure will tumble. A general who distinguished himself in the First World War writes an article on "the military weakness of Germany", filled with charts and statistics all proving German folly in waging total war.

There is something new at the front, something which is calculated to sap morale. In the First World War there had been much grumbling when "specialists" were called to the rear. Most of them, it must be admitted, were needed to work in munition plants. Yet it hurt to see comrades leave the danger zone just because they happened to be steel workers and not farmers or clerks. Moreover it became apparent very soon that many shirkers had slipped into their ranks, thanks to political or social pull. It rankled all the more when it was learned that those in the fighting line were described as P.F.W.T.F. (Poor Fools Who're at The Front).

This time those called to the rear have "special assignments". Recalls began in October, after one month of war. Certainly, some are justified. The Government, despite many speeches and schemes, never really prepared mobilisation of the industrial sector. Specialists are sorely needed. But history is repeating itself. "Special assignees" include too many shirkers. Ministers call back their friends, political bosses call back their henchmen. After three months of war many units have been deprived in this way of one third of their total. By April half have gone. The P.F.W.T.F. consist almost entirely of intellectuals, small merchants and peasants. There is much grousing.

So France – like Gaul in the days of Caesar – becomes divided into three parts. Far back there are "preservation squads" – intent chiefly on preserving their jobs and their skins. Far in front are the daredevils who roam no man's land, killing and being killed. Between them are millions of men mobilised but with nothing to do from morn till eve apart from a little drill – a sort of barrack routine in time of war. Nothing is better calculated to demoralize. Especially when men who have been on furlough return with stories of the number of young shirkers they have seen, all in fancy uniforms. Jauntily, these boys say: "Anyhow you don't need us. Up at the front there's nothing to do. Wait till you get busy and we'll join you."

They are quite correct. There is little to do at the front. Day after day the communiqué says merely: "Nothing to report". When will Hitler decide at last to commit suicide on "The Line"? Time is still working for us. True, the British contingent does not seem to increase rapidly, but the R.A.F. is working hard. True also, when a correspondent can shake off the press officer, he may learn many things. I pass some hours, unattended, with a howitzer battery keeping watch on the Rhine. The lieutenant in command says: "We are grateful to the Americans for the ambulances they are sending us, but personally I'd rather see more big guns".

On the whole this strange war continues to be regarded with apathy. Reaction lacks even when the *Revue des Deux Mondes* writes: "General Gamelin has been criticised for his inactivity during the winter. The critics are wrong, because the means at his disposal precluded fighting a great battle with hope of success. Even today we have a very steep hill to climb!" Officers and others publish detailed accounts of the operations which brought disaster to Poland. They hold out warnings destined to fall on deaf ears.

An editor writes: "It is a mental relief for the average German to place his personal destiny in the hands of the Führer. The average Frenchman has no Führer; he places his destiny in the hands of Fate." And he reads with complacency such things as this: "Always in our history a miracle man has come forth in times of stress". Why worry?

Finland is beaten. Norway is attacked. But they are so far away. Volunteers for Finland are sent to Narvik. The censor is so active that no one quite knows what it is all about. But the Premier proclaims triumphantly: "The road to iron is cut". And "The Line" still stands, stronger than ever. Let Hitler come!

He comes – on Friday, May 10 1940. Gamelin issues a general order which subsequently will be his severest condemnation: "The attack which we had foreseen since October last was launched this morning..." October was eight months ago. What has been done in these eight months? The answer soon comes. "Virtually nothing."

Instead of waiting behind their "formidable" defences the French and British advance into Belgium even into Holland. Forty-eight hours later Gamelin issues another general order: "No ground must be yielded; rather than retire, units will die on their positions". The tone is not convincing; indeed the order brings dismay to many who see in it a tragic parody of Joffre's message on the eve of the Battle of the Marne twenty-five years before. Joffre won, anyway.

The stark reality is this: the Allied armies are in full retreat. No miracle man has appeared. Weygand is called too late.

Thus begins a six-week campaign which will leave France whipped worse than by any other defeat in her history. The words are Pétain's. Politicians speak many a heroic word, soldiers do many a heroic deed. But one cannot escape from the facts:

France	Germany
85 divisions	220 divisions
3 000 tanks	22 000 tanks
5 000 airplanes	23 000 airplanes

The German host pushes on, clanging and rattling, for it is all on wheels. The roads are filled with retreating troops and fleeing citizenry. A gunner says: "How can we fire? We would kill one hundred women and children for each German". Ammunition becomes scarce. In places the retreat becomes rout. "The Line" still stands but it has lost all value. The invader is now far beyond it.

Some French radio stations continue to broadcast. During intermissions their general call is a bar from the Marseillaise: "To arms, Citizens!" The gramophone record is so worn that the phrase becomes one hoarse splutter, a tragic mockery – fit prelude to the ill tidings to follow.

The Germans push on, along roads strewn with wrecked trucks and cars. The French Government flees before them, hampered by impedimenta; it cannot reconcile itself to scrapping its files! At Amboise the Air Ministry requisitions hearses to carry its archives!

When the invader meets opposition he swerves but seldom stops. Bridges by the score are blown up in his path. But neither does that stop him; special units of bridge-builders soon restore traffic.

The die is cast. All is over. At village pumps booted Germans, stripped to the waist, remove the stains of battle. Italy seizes the moment to "declare war".

CHAPTER 16

MAGINOT AND HIS LINE

The causes of this unparalleled disaster were many, both material and moral. Outstanding among them was the Maginot Line. Devised as a tower of strength, it proved a broken reed. Why?

First a sketch of the man, then consideration of his work. It was early in the First World War, when my infantry unit was before Verdun, that I came to know André Maginot. In my battalion there was a sergeant of that name. One day we happened to meet; the Germans were shelling our billets and we had sought shelter in the same funk-hole.

"Isn't there a Deputy called Maginot?" I asked.

"Yes. He's my cousin. He's serving in the 44th, not far from here."

"Officer, I suppose? What's his rank?"

"Officer? No. He began the war as corporal and he's just been promoted sergeant. He's already won two citations. When it was left to Deputies of military age to decide their line of duty many remained in Paris. André chose the front. I go over to see him from time to time. I'll take you along one of these nights, if you like."

André Maginot struck one immediately by his great stature, near six feet six inches. That was a family trait – one of his ancestors was among the tallest of Napoleon's Grenadiers. He saw to it that there should be no corresponding girth. An

226

excellent fencer, especially with the "épée", he kept fit that way; also in winter by hunting, scouring hill and dale after hare or partridge. This stood him in good stead when war came. At that time his sandy hair was abundant, his moustache thick and long as was the fashion. Though born in Paris, with an English grandparent on the distaff side, he was a true son of Lorraine, from where his family hailed. The characteristic sing-song of the Eastern Marches was to be noted in his speech and he was stubborn, as befitted a Lorrainer. His blue eyes could become very hard.

At high school in Paris he had been in the same class with two other Andrés – Tardieu, the future Premier and Citroën the future "French Henry Ford". In the Latin Quarter later he had been the darling of the girls, but his student pranks had remained within bounds. His chance came when a friend of the family recommended him to Célestin Jonnart, Governor-General of Algeria, who gave him a position in that colony. Returning to France after some years he turned to politics. In 1910 he was elected Deputy for the Meuse Department, in Lorraine of course; three years later he was Under-Secretary for War. At the outbreak of hostilities he rejoined the 44th Territorial Infantry at Verdun as a private, second class. He was then 38 years old.

With the 44th Maginot felt at home. Most of the men were from his own province; many were his constituents. They admired him for having refused to remain at the rear and nearly everyone addressed him as "Monsieur Maginot". Within three months he had risen to corporal, then sergeant, after leading many patrols into the enemy lines. All who went with him were volunteers. Maginot himself was diffident when this subject was broached.

Not so his companions – Corporal Boury and all the privates. While Maginot and his cousin sat apart talking of home, these would tell how "Monsieur Maginot", always craving for action, had led the way into a village where there was a brush with Death-head Hussars, five of whom were killed. The sergeant himself accounted for two and brought back the leader's sabre as a trophy. They would tell also how the very next day their volunteer group had again ventured forth, with "Monsieur Maginot" surprising a German sentry.

In all, the group already had some fifty daring coups to its credit, although we were still in the winter of 1914. Yet their sergeant was always thirsty for more action. The cousin explained: "André has had sad news from Revigny (the family home) – first shelled then burned to the ground. He doesn't know what has become of his young son and daughter. He says he has a personal score to settle with the Germans." In settlement of that score he soon won another citation as well as the Military Medal; it described him as displaying not only "remarkable personal bravery" but as "having great ascendancy over his men".

He had had so many narrow escapes that he grew ever more daring, reckless even. On November 9, 1914, he was grievously wounded, nearly captured. With a party of his volunteers he crawled towards a wood. He approached within twenty yards before discovering that a superior German force was lying in ambush. A volley put four of his men out of action, then the enemy came into the open. Maginot signalled the retreat and remained alone to cover it. First a bullet hit his shin-bone and he fell. Rising again, he fired four more rounds, but a second bullet struck the knee-cap of the same leg. Nevertheless he was able to crawl to a boulder behind which he joined the remainder of his party.

It was then nine o'clock in the morning. Until nightfall the Germans repeatedly strove to capture the band but each time fell back under hot fire. In the darkness the French withdrew, bearing their sergeant with them. So helpless and heavy was he that they dragged him several miles. At the hospital amputation seemed inevitable, but two successive operations by a skilful surgeon saved the limb, although Maginot could never use it again. At the end of a year of treatment he was able to hobble on crutches, then with two sticks. The skirmish was the subject of a general order:

"Corporal Boury and First class Private Robert, of the 44th Territorials, succeeded under a hail of bullets in bringing back their wounded sergeant, after having defended him eight hours, together with the eight men whose names follow, all either killed or wounded: Privates Georges, Toussain, Boudailles, Chapelet and Gilles, killed; Privates Poilblanc, Hiblot and Degombert, wounded."

Invalided out of the Army, Maginot returned to parliamentary life, to become Cabinet Minister repeatedly. At the front he had been known as "Monsieur Maginot"; at the rear he became known as "Sergeant Maginot". He was very proud to be called by this name; it figures on the monument to his memory set up near Souville, on the battlefield of Verdun.

The next time I saw Maginot was at the Victory Parade on Bastille Day in 1919. Allied and Associated troops marched past in alphabetical order, with America first. But in front of Pershing came a pathetic group of maimed and wounded. Maginot towered above them all. He was all smiles. The sergeant had settled his score!

Maginot died in the winter of 1931, from typhoid ascribed to tainted oysters. He was given a military funeral; the colours of the 44th were there, borne exceptionally by a sergeant. During his career as Cabinet Minister a legend had grown around him and the life he led. According to his opponents he was generally in his cups and passed most of his nights at Maxim's, frequentation of which famed café, in the popular view, stamped one as a gay dog indeed. His friends indignantly denied the impeachment.

The truth lies midway, as I can testify. Maginot liked good cheer; he was a judge of wine – and of women. And he did not conceal the fact that he played a good hand at poker. At the front, to my knowledge, he did not despise a drop of good brandy. Few of us did for that matter. After the war, to my knowledge also, his preference was for Voisin's Restaurant, now defunct, where they knew his tastes in food and drink.

Politically he may have been a hard foe, but as a man he had his points. For one thing he dressed well – but there are people who consider white spats a sign of snobbishness. Maginot may not have been a great man, but he was a man – at a time when they were few.

Now for the Maginot Line; even here the French could not eschew party lines and labels. At the outset of his political career André Maginot inclined towards the Left; at its peak he inclined towards the Right. So that the Left came to object to the designation: "Maginot Line". Some newspapers made a point of calling it: "The Painlevé-Maginot Line". They had one great argument to support their point. Indubitably Paul Painlevé was Minister of War when that system of fortification was approved and experimental construction began. But going further back one may find an official letter dated February 25, 1919, written by Georges Clemenceau as Minister of War to Marshal Pétain as Commander-in-chief of the French Army, suggesting a line of fortified works along the Eastern frontier.

Why not therefore a Clemenceau-Pétain-Painlevé-Maginot Line? Or, more simply, a Belhague Line, from the name of the general in the Engineering Corps chiefly responsible for building it?

However all that may be, Maginot Line remains the accepted popular term and Maginot Line it is likely to remain. André Maginot may not have conceived it, he may not have built it; he did infinitely more under conditions of a Parliamentary Republic – he obtained the necessary appropriations! The conception was still in the germinal stage when in 1929 Maginot, just appointed Minister of War, investigated on the spot, found work hampered by lack of funds, and to the end of his life devoted himself to the single task of completing it.

Today Maginot's sincerity is unquestioned. His purpose was to build a dam against eventual German aggression. He had no part in elaborating a military doctrine which made of the Maginot Line the be all and end all. It was to be everything; it turned out to be nothing. And it fostered a dangerous delusion because it was designed for defence at a time when French foreign policy should have been all for offence if succour were really to be given to allies and associates.

Which does not prevent the Maginot Line from having been a wonderful piece of machinery, a military wonder. The engineers had foreseen every contingency, save one, which after all was not their business. If attacked form the rear, "The Line" had no defence and was woefully vulnerable. Otherwise each "work" was well-nigh perfect. Work ("ouvrage") was the official name for constructions without precedent in the art of fortification. They were really warships sunk deep into the earth. So true was the simile that the garrisons were called "crews", divided into "watches". The men slept in bunks, sometimes in hammocks. But there were no decks where the salt spray whips the blood, and conditions told on health – artificial air, artificial light, artificial water even, all very scientific but utterly unnatural. Your fighting-man is not a hothouse plant!

The topography of the land had been so well studied and so well utilised that, viewed from the German side, the untrained eye could have seen nothing but rolling country had it not been for rusty barbed wire and tank traps, obviously too wide for cattle fences. Although they were camouflaged to match the grass, the expert could discern rings betraying the tops of turrets. Generally the "works" were far from habitations; under the grey skies of the Marshes they seemed stern and forbidding.

At the rear, facing France, the resemblance was with a tenement building – metal ladders, garbage cans, and washing out to dry; at some distance, chicken coops, rabbit hutches, a few shacks, possibly a cabbage patch. The only reminder of a military purpose was a ponderous steel hatch, destined to close upon the defenders on the day of battle. Their mission was to fight entombed and to justify the motto on their badges: "No one may pass!" No one did, for that matter. The enemy went round to rap at the back-door.

In its way the Maginot Line was an assemblage of gadgets. I recall visiting a minor "work" where a sergeant proudly did the honours of his turret. Three tiers. Above, two men, each at a heavy machine-gun; their work was automatic, not much more complicated than pressing the trigger, since the pieces were laid immutably and all ranges were shown on a photographic panorama revolving with the turret. In the middle tier, the sergeant and an assistant with appliances of all kinds –

periscope, telescope, telemeter. Below, two men to work the turret and assure an even flow of ammunition. It was all very compact, very efficient, and very impressive. The sergeant beamed when told so.

"There's one thing more I want to show you", he said. "See this switch!" he grew eloquent as he conjured up visions of his turret in action. "All that the boys above have got to do is shoot, shoot, shoot. But they might get so excited that they wouldn't stop or, if we brought up reserves, they might not distinguish between friend and foe. In that case I work the switch. And lo! Their guns are locked."

There were innumerable contrivances in "The Line" – to prevent embrasures from being blocked with earth thrown up by enemy shells, to avoid condensation of moisture, to divert slops deep into the subsoil. No detail was overlooked. This was essential, since each "work" was intended to act independently once battle was joined. Each had to become self-sustained and self-contained – a microcosm with kitchen, bakery and rations for many days; reserves of water, wells, filters; a power station with capacious fuel tanks; a telephone exchange and wireless connection; a ventilation system, with appliances to fight poison-gas; central heating for winter, fans for summer; hospital, pharmacy, operating-room; elevators for men and for material; magazines for ammunition; laundry and drying-closets; rails for miniature cars in the many galleries; workshops with stores for spare parts; drainage and plumbing – and miles of piping and wiring. In every sense at once a buried city and a volcano ready to belch forth.

All weapons, all appliances were controlled from the command post, deep in the bowels of the earth, recalling the mummy chamber of an Egyptian tomb. Thereon converged also all the wires and all the pipes. Enamelled white, brilliantly

233

illuminated, the post presented an uncanny sight with its walls covered with charts, diagrams, dials and switches. In action, several officers and sergeants watched them all attentively or listened to telephone and radio, while lamps of many colours glowed and faded again, each with a meaning. And the silence was as of the tomb, apart from occasional terse orders, for the tumult and the shouting was unable to reach these depths.

The commander saw nothing of the world above, yet he sensed all. Every pulsation of the land-ship was conveyed to him instantly – and he reacted instantly. He was in touch also with adjoining "works", whose fire interlocked; few cannons, but many machine-guns and anti-tanks guns. And he reported periodically to his chiefs far behind, who disposed of mobile troops for counter-attack. When he glanced at his badge he saw the words: "No one may pass!" and he believed them.

But in those June days in 1940 the Germans crossed the Rhine on the East and came through Luxemburg and Belgium on the West. Mobile troops were withdrawn and "The Line" stood alone – to serve no end. Some crews refused to surrender, even after the Armistice, until ordered by radio to cease their unavailing fire.

The Maginot Line became but a memory. Never its like will be seen again. Which is well probably. From a fetish it had become a cloak to cover many errors – and not a few lies.

CHAPTER 17

"A LIE CANNOT LIVE!"

No one can tell when it will be possible to write accurately and impartially of this brief campaign, tragic beyond words. Even today details lack regarding the War of 1914-18. For example the precise day and hour of Joffre's historic order on the eve of the Battle of the Marne have yet to be determined. After twenty years and more, some documents are still withheld for personal, political or other reasons. How then can one hope to unravel the tangled skein of yesterday? And it is to be feared that many a historian will sink many times in a slough of lies before reaching the well into which Truth was forced back, with a heavy weight on the cover.

It is a lamentable reflection on democracy, French democracy at least, as well as confirmation of its impotence, that for years, under governments of all shades, it could seldom know the truth. All conspired to conceal it – supine bureaucracy, mendacious communiqués, speeches of many words and little substance, tacit complicity of the press. In time of peace this was sufficient of a crime; in time of war it is rank treason. In war moreover the censor came to draw the veil still further. Lies certainly hastened the fall of France.

Censorship was normal and acceptable in its initial purpose of preventing dissemination of intelligence likely to serve the enemy. But very soon it stood revealed as an all too convenient instrument for concealing unpleasant facts, directing opinion into predetermined grooves, and suppressing criticism.

From military censorship there grew offshoots – political, economic, diplomatic – each more noxious than the other.

I have had considerable experience of French censors. In private life and individually they might be charming men, intelligent and enlightened; professionally and collectively they are obtuse, ridiculous, ever afraid of assuming responsibility. Few, very few, endeavoured to understand the reasons prompting instructions they received; the majority preferred the line of least resistance and used the blue pencil indiscriminately. Had they been told to eliminate "indications of localities and names of persons", they would have treated the Lord's Prayer thus: "Ours ---- which art in -----, hallowed be thy -----, thy ----- come". With such mentality the road is open to every abuse.

The United States has been fortunate in this respect, thanks to its institutions, thanks also to its newspapers. The American press has its faults, but it has a redeeming sense of civic duty. The nation, moreover, not only expects news but demands it, and normally it does not accept official reticence. So that it was possible to bring together publishers and censors, representing the public on the one hand and the government on the other. A measure of control was accepted, in return for an undertaking that news, accurate and uncoloured, would be available in due course. Of all communiqués during this war the Americans have proved the most objectively frank. The report on the Battle of Midway issued in July 1942 stands as a model.

The value of French official reports may be gauged from what information the press vouchsafed on operations. The system was typified by what was known as "the Thomas Conference". Each day Lieutenant-Colonel E.T. Thomas assembled reporters, correspondents and "military experts" at the Ministry of War in Paris. In periods of activity on the front there were two sessions, morning and evening; otherwise morning only. The setting was a large room, high ceilinged, with trophies of arms on the walls. Curtains were drawn over the large windows and all was done by artificial light – a symbol perhaps.

The ostensible purpose was to explain and amplify the communiqués issued twice daily from G.H.Q.; in practise Colonel Thomas' mission was to make a great show of producing a powerful searchlight, but omitting to turn on the switch. Communiqués were invariably terse, generally forty-eight hours behind the events, frequently cryptic, occasionally misleading. The colonel's explanations and amplifications, so called, followed the same lines under the guise of frankness. Considered in retrospect – I attended most of these conferences – it is clear that the whole truth was rarely told. Three or four communiqués drafted by General Maxime Weygand himself were exceptions, but it is only too obvious now that in the majority of instances the Government controlled all news of operations. Doubtless that was its prerogative, but it was a factor in its undoing. For if military sources tended to delay imparting information in the hope that a few hours more might change the situation, the civil authority tended to distort facts so that they might match with its policy.

On occasion both military and civil sources would conspire to lie deliberately. A painful example occurred in February 1940. On the 19th of that month the morning communique reported: "East of the Nied one of our detachments fell into an ambush during the night and suffered losses." Allowing for its reticence this announcement was perfectly accurate. But Colonel Thomas ventured to elaborate, with the consequence that several newspapers printed explanations purporting to show that the detachment in question had pushed far into the enemy lines, "emboldened probably by previous successes", and had fallen victim to its ardour. One account added: "The Commander-in-Chief, even before knowing all the details, insisted on making an announcement.

237

This attitude gives greater value to our communiqués, the accuracy of which cannot be denied by the enemy who, on the contrary, always tends to exaggerate." The censor, of course, let that pass; he must have regretted it.

For two days later it was admitted that the ambush had cost the French some thirty men – heavy loss at a time when fighting was confined to patrols and when the Government seized every occasion to insist that casualties were virtually negligible. Further explanation was necessary. So the story was printed that an inexperienced second lieutenant, in command of a relief in trucks, had lost his way in the darkness and entered enemy territory, where the party was attacked and virtually wiped out. The report ended: "The unfortunate officer paid for his error with his life".

It happened that soon afterwards I went on a visit to the front. I found officers there indignant, especially in subaltern ranks. They complained bitterly that the lieutenant's memory had been tarnished and they gave quite another version. The Germans had ambushed the party far within the French lines. There had been no recklessness on the part of the young officer, who had done his duty to the end, but he had been made a scapegoat in order to conceal the enemy's enterprise.

This version was correct. Two months passed. Then, the incident having been forgotten Second Lieutenant Jean Babelot – the officer in question - was awarded the Croix de Guerre posthumously and his memory was cleared. But the general public never knew. The fiction of a "strange" war was maintained…

Lieutenant-Colonel Thomas was always punctual – an exception among French officials – always courteous. That he was intelligent was proved by the fact that, while seeming to tell much, in reality he told nothing. His conferences were attended by several retired generals, among them Charles Brécard, Julien Brossé and Maurice Duval, all of whom wrote interpretative articles in various newspapers. Among non-military commentators stood out Lucien Romier, of the *Figaro*, later to become one of Marshal Pétain's Ministers of State. Brécard, who wrote in the *Jour*, which has now ceased publication, was for a time Pétain's secretary-general, then Grand Chancellor of the Order of the Legion of Honour. A cavalry man, he had played a prominent part in the First World War at the head of various dismounted divisions. Brossé wrote for the *Temps* with discernment. But the keenest brain at these conferences was Duval, who contributed to the *Journal* in the morning and the *Journal des Débats* in the evening.

A sparse man with drooping white moustache, Duval invariably came with a brief-case filled with documents. He also had distinguished himself in the First World War. On taking supreme command, Pétain entrusted him with reorganisation of the Air Force. When the Germans broke through the British Fifth Army and threatened Amiens, it was he who conceived and directed the first air attack against infantry. In fact his pilots, flying low and machine-gunning, filled the breach between the French and British armies until reinforcements could arrive. Duval subsequently, impressed by German might, wrote admiringly of the Axis.

At the Thomas conferences General Duval generally remained silent. A few days before the Government fled from Paris, however, he broke out in intense indignation: "Colonel", he said in effect, "the public in general and Parisians in particular are not at all satisfied with the information we give them, which after all is merely the information you give us. They are not quite as simple as to believe what we are induced to tell them. I live near the Bois de Boulogne. Like everyone else I have seen trenches and anti-tank defences prepared there in recent days. This morning no fewer than four women I know stopped me to ask what it all meant. My vague reply that these were mere measures of precaution failed to convince. The women shook their heads and said: 'It means that the Germans are very near!' We all sense that they are right. What France wants is the truth. And France is not getting it. What are you going to do about it?"

Thomas flushed but otherwise remained as imperturbable as ever. "I can tell you only what I am instructed to tell you" he implied. His stock phrase at the time was: "The situation is admittedly serious but it is not desperate". General Duval's friends were right, of course. "The truth will be out, even in an affidavit" - even in a war communiqué. Not many days later correspondents assembled one morning to discover that Colonel Thomas had gone. The previous evening he had said as usual: "See you tomorrow, gentlemen". But he had flitted with the Government. At Tours the conferences were resumed, to be told once again that "serious, even very serious" did not necessarily mean "desperate". "See you tomorrow", Thomas concluded. On the morrow the colonel was off to Bordeaux with the Government. There the farce ended; there were no more Thomas conferences. Everybody in France knew what was happening without need of explanation or amplification.

When correspondents, by deduction or intuition, did succeed in lifting the veil so sedulously lowered by Lieutenant-Colonel Thomas, acting on instructions, the censor was there to call a halt. In Paris a fact or two, or at least a hint or two, could occasionally be slipped into despatches. At the front never. Under the plea of "higher interests of national defence", anything and everything could be deleted. And the officer-censors at G.H.Q. were generally curt if not downright arrogant. One wondered why such men were chosen for such posts; certainly it was not because of special qualifications. Most of them belonged to the Reserve. There was every reason to believe that they owed their jobs either to political or social "pull" and that they had been clever enough to secure their assignments long before the war began. The real purpose of certain associations, all placed under the patronage of prominent politicians, became only too clear.

These men seemed intent on impressing all and sundry that G.H.Q. was the holy of holies and that each officer there was invested with at least a crumb of the authority of the Commander-in-Chief. On one of my visits to the front I was authorised by General André Prételat, commanding Army Group No.1, to see a "nomad battery" of 105mm guns in action near the lines north of Metz. Out on the snow-covered hills, tractors rapidly brought the guns. The objective was artillery emplacements far on the German side of the lines. As soon as ranges had been given, shell after shell whined through the still air. Sixty rounds were fired in short order. Then the tractors returned to remove the guns before the enemy could locate their positions and reply in kind. It was all over in a few minutes and we were two miles away before the first German shell burst. Very efficient and not a little dramatic.

In my despatch I referred vaguely to a battery on a hill near a wood, without further precision. At G.H.Q. a captain took it in hand and promptly blue-pencilled "hill" and "wood". I protested: "Why can't these words go, Captain?"

"Because no indication of localities is permitted to pass, as you ought to know."

"But, Captain, this is Lorraine and in Lorraine there is nothing but hills and woods. I mention no place-names in this despatch, only 'a hill' or 'a wood'. Surely ..."

"I'm the censor, not you. This is a matter of national defence interest and that's all there is to it."

No wonder the French were in a stupor when defeat became evident. They had been allowed to know nothing of the war beyond the picture-book side. For eight months this presentation had been possible, even plausible, for in reality there had been no war. When on May 10 it began in dead earnest, stupor began also. It was too late to turn the page of the picture-book. Events moved too swiftly. How could it all have happened? There was no time to answer then. The stupor grew.

Adolf Hitler gave his explanation to the Reichstag on July 19. He said:

"Concentration facing Belgium of all the British and French motorised forces made it appear certain that the Allied armies were intended to enter that country at the earliest. Since I could rest entire confidence in the German infantry divisions engaged in that sector, any blows struck by us on the right flank of the Franco-British motorised army corps were calculated to entail its destruction and probably its encirclement.

Contrary to the Schlieffen Plan of 1914, I transferred to the left wing of my front the centre of gravity of this operation. The success of this feint is due only to having given an impression of an intention to do the contrary."

Which reads very smoothly – after the event. It is possible that history will reveal this explanation as belonging also to the picture-book school. The truth seems rather to take a middle course. The German High Command had a plan, the French had not. Grouped behind the Maginot Line and the field fortifications prolonging it to the North Sea, the French ascribed superior value to static defence. Therein resided their entire plan. The Maginot Line having become a symbol, nothing else entered into consideration. Thus confined, military imagination ascribed all sorts of impossibility to dynamism, to daring use of airplanes and tanks, to movement or to manoeuvre. The

Germans, on the other hand, had retained faith in the offensive. Furthermore they had created means to that end.

There is the story in a nutshell. That and the lack of preparation. To which must be added a policy so blind that it surpasses understanding. Ever since the peace of Versailles in 1919, the French, as we have seen, pursued diplomatic and military ends so divergent, so contradictory that they could not fail to bring disaster. Diplomatic policy demanded the offensive, yet military policy remained entirely defensive. Diplomacy, so far as it existed at all, sought alliances, mutual pacts of security, aid to and from certain States, all of which implied the creation of an army ready at all times to operate beyond the frontier. Yet military policy remained stubbornly static. For years it was based on "national defence" and nothing more. So much so that when war became a virtual certainty, the Minister of War serenely changed his title to Minister of National Defence. The climax was reached in this paradox: a defensive war to aid Poland, separated from France by hundreds of miles and by the territories of several other states!

France pledged herself to aid in Europe the "Little Entente", Poland, Belgium, Holland, Switzerland and others, yet her whole military plan was to wait behind the Maginot Line! True, on September 3, when the Germans had already penetrated far into Poland, the Army advanced in the direction of the Westwall. The Germans were scarcely disturbed. Soon the army which had figuratively gone up the hill came down again, back to the Maginot Line. The next months were spent extending and strengthening that line until it was proclaimed "formidable". Then, on May 10, the army marched off again, into Belgium and Holland. Within twenty-four hours it was reeling. In September 1939 the French had advanced and then retired because of lack of material; eight months later they again advanced and were defeated, also because of lack of material.

By May 13 the 9th French Army, under General André Corap, which held a key position on the Meuse, had been "volatilised", to quote Paul Reynaud's tremulous broadcast. The hunt for scapegoats had begun, to lead eventually to a trial for "responsibilities" before a Supreme Court specially set up for the purpose. Corap was chosen as the first, but when the time came his peers absolved him. Taking into account the paltry means afforded him, he could scarcely have done better. Moreover General Charles Huntziger's 2nd Army also had let the Germans through – at Sedan, on Corap's right flank. Who was the more to blame? And in what measure was the High Command responsible? Moreover, who would have presumed to decide, seeing that Huntziger had become Minister of War? It is still a matter of controversy whether Joffre or Gallieni won the Battle of the Marne in 1914; it may long be discussed whether Corap or Huntziger lost the Battle of the Meuse.

In any event, apportionment of responsibility had no purpose then, for a breach fifty miles wide had been made in the French line and the enemy poured through it armoured and motorised divisions one after the other. On May 13 the war was virtually lost for the French; the breach never could be filled. All efforts to do so merely moved it westward, ever westward to the sea. The roads to Dunkirk were strewn with abandoned equipment. That was the Battle of Flanders. The Battle of France followed thereafter.

"Our Gamelin" had been removed with ignominy – another scapegoat. Others were sought – the Belgians, the British. What mattered most then was to perpetuate the lies fed to the people. The question of asking for an armistice had actually been mooted; the Government rejected it. It preferred to explain all setbacks by "defections" and to conceal the full extent of the defeat in Flanders.

So General Maxime Weygand was summoned post-haste from the Middle East to take supreme command of the Allied forces and the fate of France was placed in the hands of a man of 73! True, Weygand had remained young in body and in spirit. His immediate concern was to appraise the situation at first-hand. Through anti-aircraft barrages an Army airplane bore him to the front, then to the coast whence a destroyer brought him to a safe port; then back to Paris to report to the Government. At the Ministry of War officers and soldiers would snap to attention while civilians bared their heads as the spare figure passed in and out. But what could Weygand do? He had been called too late. Colonel Thomas, the while, at his daily conference, steadfastly instilled hope into the communiqués!

By that time practically the whole of the French forces had been engaged. The country still imagined there were reserves. The High Command knew better – the Germans also, doubtless. From left to right it was still possible to transfer units to fill vital gaps, but these reinforcements never consisted of fresh troops. The French were definitely outnumbered and out-powered. The only hope was to save honour on the one hand and to preserve homogeneity of units on the other in order to prevent retreat from degenerating into rout.

Weygand had sent the Government three reports, all urgent: one at the end of May, the other two early in June. All tended to show that a request for an armistice had become inevitable. It was no longer a war, only a massacre. The last came on June 12 and 13. Paris was not yet occupied then, the Loire was not crossed. Much might have been saved. But Paul Reynaud demurred because "public opinion was not prepared". Hitherto public opinion had been disregarded.

So for a full week more men were killed and the German columns advanced further and further. The government was then in Bordeaux, evidently out of touch with the country.

Paul Reynaud's dramatic appeal from Tours to the United States had come to nought, as everyone - probably himself included – knew it would.

All was chaos. Not that the entire army was routed. There were many examples of desperate resistance which compelled admiration, even from the enemy. Groups of determined men held back the invader for hours, if not for days. For a whole month, the 2nd Cavalry Division was in the breach, first on the Channel coast, then in the West, under a gallant commander, General André Berniquet. He was killed "on the evening of the last day" in a small village. The German command authorised all his surviving officers to attend the funeral.

There was the 114th Infantry Regiment, disbanded after the First World War and hastily formed again on May 28 from stragglers of Corap's Army "volatilised" on the Meuse. Improvised and without cohesion, this unit was nevertheless thrown into the fray on June 7 near Forges-les-Eaux which a German armoured division was threatening after having, according to French accounts, "dispersed British troops near Abbeville". Thrown back on Formelie, the regiment held there three days, until overwhelmed. When it was all over, the German general sent for the French commander and said: "Since the campaign opened I never met such resistance. We imagined you were more numerous and better armed."

There was the 92nd Infantry Regiment, belonging to the 25th Division which covered the retreat in Flanders and, in particular, defended Lille. The men who returned scarcely formed a company; all the others were killed, wounded or taken prisoner. Those captured at Lille were accorded the honours of war; they were allowed to march through the occupied city, retaining their arms and flying their colours.

There were the Cavalry Cadets of the famous school at Saumur. For two days they prevented passage across the Loire. Afterwards the German general said: "We believed we had an entire division against us".

Several days before the end of hostilities, the French forces had been utterly cut up and each section isolated, ever outdistanced and outflanked by tanks and airplanes. One division – the 20th – after holding the Moselle sector for many months, fought rear-guard actions as far as Château-Thierry. The enemy had progressed so swiftly that when the division reached the Seine, its orders were to fight facing south!

There were many other examples of gallantry and of sacrifice. But nothing could avail. A lie cannot live. And near two million men, the flower of French manhood, went to Germany as prisoners.

BIOGRAPHICAL DETAILS

GASTON HANET ARCHAMBAULT

Born 25/02/1877 in Ay, France.
Died 21/05/1951 in Cape Town, South Africa
French citizen
Wrote and published in both English and French

1894-1898   *Bedfordshire Times & Independent*, based in Bedford, England – articled to editor

1898-1901   National service in the French Army, Nancy France

1901-1904   *The Daily Messenger*, Paris – Assistant sub-editor to Ralph Lane (who was later awarded the Nobel Peace Prize under the name Norman Angell)

1903-1904   weekly letter in *Manchester Sunday Chronicle*

1904-1914   The Paris *Herald* – Editor in charge under James Gordon Bennett Jr (European edition of the *New York Herald*)

1914-1918   WW1 in French Army, wounded in battle and awarded the Legion d'Honneur for action in Verdun

1917-1918   Liaison Officer to American Expeditionary Forces

1919-1924   The Paris *Herald* – Editor in charge under Frank Munsey

1924-1929   *The Paris Times* – founder

1929-1939 Writes from Paris for many newspapers as freelance journalist (sometimes under the pen name Cyril Alexander) including *The Sun, Chicago Daily News, Dayton Daily News, Morning News, The Spectator, The New York Times*

1939-1945 WW2 frontline correspondent for *The New York Times* based in Paris, Vichy and in Bern Switzerland (many of his articles made front page news)

1946-1951 South Africa correspondent for *The New York Times* based in Pretoria

EDUCATION
Schooling at Hornsey and Bedford Modern School, England

PUBLICATIONS
"*L'Origine des Nouvelles*" Mercure de France Sept 1935

"*Take Heed America*" Woolly Whale Press June 1941

"*Europe in Turmoil and Democracy in Peril 1900-1940 – My life as a newspaper man, from The Herald to The New York Times*" written in 1942, the manuscript was recently discovered, to be published 2023

ACKNOWLEDGEMENTS

This book was written in 1942 when the tide of war seemed to be turning and hope for the Allies returned. The manuscript lay forgotten for many years and was rediscovered in our family papers in 2008.

Although there is no sign of this, it would have been logical for the author to follow up with a sequel to this book covering WWII and drawing upon the hundreds of articles he wrote for *The New York Times* as front line correspondent. These articles may be consulted in the NYT archives *https://timesmachine.nytimes.com* by searching for G.H. Archambault.

However we do know that after WWII GHA was working on a different book, "The Origin of News", which was to be an account of the development of newspapers and of journalism. He published an article in French in 1935 on this subject.

Gaston Hanet Archambault was my grandfather.

Many thanks to my sister Kari Hanet for rediscovering the manuscript and for typing it up.

Peter Hanet, email hanetp@aol.com

Printed in Great Britain
by Amazon

40175864R00139